白

原研哉

中央公論新社

白

まえがき

白について語ることは色彩について語ることではない。それは自分たちの文化の中にあるはずの感覚の資源を探り当てていく試みである。つまり、簡潔さや繊細さを生み出す美意識の原点を、白という概念の周辺に探ってみたのである。

僕はデザイナーという仕事をしている。専門はコミュニケーションである。だから「もの」ではなく「こと」を作っている。具体的にはポスターやパッケージ、シンボルマークやブックデザイン、そして展覧会などを無数に作ってきたが、それらは言わば「こと」の痕跡のようなものだ。いかに印象的に記憶されるか、いかに鮮烈にイメージを屹立させられるか、つまり、世の中や人の頭の中に、どうすれば特別な結び目を作ることができるかを考えながら仕事をしてきた。そういう仕事を繰り返すうちに、自分だけではない、おそらくは日本の、あるいは世界の文化の中に蓄積されてきた意思疎通の知恵、あるいはツボのようなものが意識されてくるのである。

そのうちのひとつに「空/エンプティネス」、すなわち「空っぽ」という概念がある。人と意思の疎通を行う時には、一方的に情報を投げかけるのではなく、むしろ相手

のイメージを受け入れる方が有効である場合が多い。つまりいかに多く説得したかではなく、いかに多く聞けたかが、コミュニケーションの質を左右する。だから人々は、歴史の中では、時に意図的に空っぽの器のようなものを作って、コミュニケーションを図ってきた。たとえば、日の丸や十字架などの簡潔きわまりないシンボルは、何かの意味を担う限定的な記号というよりも、それに触れた人々が生み出す多様なイメージの全てを引き受け、受容する大きな空っぽの器のようなものだ。巨大な墳墓や教会などの空間、あるいは茶室や庭なども、そういうもののひとつである。したがって、当初は「空(うつ)」について書こうとしていた。しかし、書き進むうちに「白」にたどり着いた。「白」は「空白」などという言葉があるように、「空」に深く関係したのである。「空」を掘り進む上では避けて通れない対象物のように思われた。だから「空」を書く前にこちらを先に書いてみることにしたのである。

この本を読んだあなたは、もはや「白」が簡単に白くは見えなくなるかもしれない。あるいは本当に白いものはより輝きを増して感じられるはずだ。それは、あなたの感覚の目盛りが、少し細かくなった証拠である。白を感知する感度が上がった分だけ、世界は陰翳の度をも増すはずであるから。

まえがき ——————————————————————— i

第一章　白の発見 ——————————————————— 1

白は感受性である／色とは何か／いとしろし／色をのがれる／情報と生命の原像

第二章　紙 ——————————————————————— 13

いとしろしき触発力／白い枚葉として／創造意欲をかき立てる媒質／反芻する白／白い四角い紙／言葉を畳む／文字というもの／活字とタイポグラフィ

第三章　空白　エンプティネス　37

空白の意味／長谷川等伯　松林図屏風／
満ちる可能性としての空白／
伊勢神宮と情報／何も言わない／
白地に赤い丸の受容力／空と白／
茶の湯／和室の原形／
発想は空白に宿る／独創的な問いに答は不要

第四章　白へ　67

推敲／白への跳躍／
清掃／未知化／白砂と月光

あとがき　78

著者自装

第一章

白の発見

白は感受性である

白があるのではない。白いと感じる感受性があるのだ。だから白を探してはいけない。白いと感じる感じ方を探るのだ。白という感受性を探ることによって、僕らは普通の白よりももう少し白い白に意識を通わせることができるようになる。そして日本の文化の中に、驚くべき多様さで織り込まれている白に気づくことができる。静けさや空白の言葉が分かるようになり、そこに潜在する意味を聞き分けられるようになる。白に気を通わせることで世界は光を増し陰翳の度を深めるのである。

活字の黒さは、文字の黒さではなく紙の白と一対になって黒い。日の丸が赤いのは、丸の赤さだけではなく地の白によって赤が輝くのだ。青であれベージュであれ、余白ならば白を内在させている。不在は存在を希求するために時として存在よりも強い存在感がある。白は汚れやすく、きれいなまま持続させることが難しいゆえに、はかなさを切なく思う心情によってより強く美しさとして印象づけられる。

このような白を介在する意識の動きに呼応するようにして、日本の建築や空間、

そして書物や庭が生まれた。かつて谷崎潤一郎はその著書『陰翳礼讃』の中で、日本文化の美意識を陰翳から語り起こした。日本の美意識を見立てていく透視図の消失点を陰翳に見る発想は秀逸であるが、翳りに対照をなす明度の極点に、もうひとつの消失点があるのではないか。そんな風に僕は思うのだ。

色とは何か

白は色だろうか。色のようだが色ではないようにも思われる。そもそも色とは何か。近代物理学の成果として今日、色彩のメカニズムは明快なシステムとして整理されている。マンセルやオストワルドの表色系と呼ばれる色の体系がそれである。明度、彩度、色相、つまり明るさや鮮やかさの度合い、そして円環をなすスペクトルによって、三次元の立体として表現された色の体系は、物理現象としての色の構造を分かりやすく理解に導いてくれる。しかしながら、人は色をこの仕組みに照らして感じているわけではない。割った卵からこぼれる濃い黄味のつややかさや、湯呑みに満ちるお茶の色合いは、単に色彩だけではなく物質性をともなった質感であり、味やにおいとの関係も深い。そういうものを複合して人は色を感じている。そういう意味では色は視覚的なものだけではなく、全感覚的なものである。表色系は、複合的

な色の中から、物理的、視覚的な性質だけを取り出してまとめられたものである。

現在、印刷や繊維、工業製品などの色を指定するための指標として色の見本帖が用いられている。これらはもっぱらマンセルやオストワルドの表色系に準じたものが大半であり、実際に色を探したり指定したりする時にはこれが便利である。間違いのない色の伝達にはこのような秩序と客観性が助けになる。

一方で、僕がよく用いる色見本帖の中に「日本の伝統色」というものがある。これは日本の伝統的な色の名前から編集された見本帖である。体系の整合性を目的に編集されたものではないので色の厳密な指定には必ずしも適してはいないが、色彩をふわりと想像させるイメージの喚起力には定評がある。この見本帖に触れると、言葉でとらえられた色の性質をすんなりと自然に受け入れられるのである。それと同時に、感覚の微細なところが目覚めてくるような寂しさをも覚える。この感慨の根は何だろうか。故郷の言葉を聞くような安心感、さらにはそこはかとない寂しさをも覚える。この感慨の根は何だろうか。

細やかな色の情緒が表現されていることはもちろんだが、それだけではない。感慨の核心は、色は人によって「見出された」ものであるということへの気づきと、その見立ての視点に共振する感動ではないだろうか。色はあらかじめ分離独立して自然の中にあるものではなく、変化する微妙な光のうつろいの中から言葉で絶妙に輪郭を与えられた性質である。その見立ての適切さに感じ入るのだ。伝統色とは、

色のとらえ方や味わい方が「色の名」という言葉として文化の中に蓄えられてきたものである。

色を想像する時に、僕らはすでに手にした色彩に対する通念を一度捨て、零に戻してそれを想像し直してみる必要があるかもしれない。日本語の「いろ」の語源は「恋人」のことでもあり、僕らが今日抱いている色彩という観念よりももっと広範囲の意味を内蔵していたようである。僕らは幸か不幸か物心ついた時にすでに十二色の色鉛筆でお絵描きをしており、水色や肌色という概念を、そこからおのずと獲得してしまっている。しかし、もしもそういう指標がまるでなく、色を名指す言葉がずっと少なかったとしたら、今のように世界の色を識別し得たであろうか。

古代、万葉の時代には、色の形容はずっと少なかったと言われている。日本語の色の形容は、赤い／黒い／白い／青い／という、下に「い」がついて形容詞となる四つであったそうだ。黄色いとか茶色いは、下に「色」が付されているので例外とする。古代に生まれた四つの形容詞はそれぞれ、明るく勢いのある様／暗く光のない様／顕しい輝き／茫漠とした印象／を形容している。四つは少ないように感じるが、おそらくは言葉の守備範囲が広く、用いられる文脈で指し示す意味や風情の微妙な差異を表現できたであろうし、また、色というものの識別が今日のような厳密さで存在する必要もなく、ブルーもグリーンも総じて青いという心情で包含でき

白｜白の発見

いたのかもしれない。他の色名は、受け手の心理を含んだ形容語というよりも、藍や紫などの植物染料の名前や、橙、灰、若草など、その色を体現している対象物の名称に即して生まれたと考えられる。

日本の伝統色がめくるめく多様性として見出されていくのは、平安の王朝文化においてである。自然のうつろいを細やかにとらえ、それを衣類や調度の色に託して表現し交感していく文化がこの時代に育まれた。季節のうつろいを四季と呼ぶが、中国の暦法から移入した二十四節気、七十二候という分類を日本は自分たちの感性に添わせた形で運用していく。一年を五日ほどの周期に分けて雪月花の微妙な変化に目を凝らしていくことがこの時代の教養であり、それを見事に詩で表現できる人が教養のある人とされた。

「萌黄」や「浅葱」など自然の色のうつろいをとらえた言葉は繊細でか弱いが、色を見出していく視点は的確で説得力を持っている。だから人の感性の深みにすっと入り込む。それは色の名という糸のついた猛烈に細い針のようなもので、僕らの感覚の敏感な部分をたやすく的確に縫う。胸に込み上げてくるのはまさに標的を射抜かれた快感あるいは共感である。さらに言えば、それらの繊細な感受性が現代の生活環境の中で消滅しつつあることを同時に悟り、せつない気分におそわれることも感慨の一部である。

ぽとりぽとりとしたたり落ちる雫の、一滴一滴の気の遠くなるような反復から「鍾乳洞」が形作られていくように、人が自然の輝きや世界のうつろいに向き合った時に生まれる心象が、少しずつ堆積して色の名前となる。あるものは失われ、あるものは変化を遂げながら、いつしかそれは色という大きな意識の体系をなしている。おそらく伝統色という色の体系は世界中に、言語や文化の数だけあるだろう。「日本の伝統色」もそのひとつである。

いとしろし

日本の伝統色における白は、古代に生まれた四つの色の形容語のひとつ「しろし」に由来する。しろしとは「いとしろし＝いちじるし」であり、顕在性を表現している。純度の高い光、水の雫にたたえられる清澄さのようなもの、あるいは、勢いよく落ちる滝のような鮮烈な輝きを持つものなど、いちじるしきものの様相は、変転する世界の中にくっきりと浮かび上がる。そういうものに意識の焦点を合わせ、感覚の琴線を震わせる心象が「しろし」である。それを言葉で捕まえ、長い歴史の中でひとつの美意識として立ち上ってきた概念が「白」である。

伝統色とは単に物理的な光の属性を言うものでなく、それ以外の多くの質や感受

性を同時に運ぶものであることは、既に述べてきた通りだが、この「白」という言葉に潜在する「いちじるし」という特性は白を読み解いていく上で大切な手がかりとなる。

色をのがれる

一方で、白は「色の不在」を表現している点でひときわ特殊な色である。ことが起こる前の、潜在の領域にあるものの状態を昔の日本人は「機前(きぜん)」と呼んだそうだ。白は発色の未然形であり、言わば機前の色である。

光の色を全て混ぜあわせると白になり、絵の具やインクの色を全て引いていくと白になる。白はあらゆる色の総合であると同時に無色である。色をのがれる点で特別な色である。別な言い方をすれば、白は色であることにとどまらない。色をのがれた分だけより強く物質性を喚起させる質感であり、間や余白のような時間性や空間性をはらむものでいる。ここで述べる白は流行色のように消費される色の属性でもなく、不在やゼロ度のような抽象的な概念をも含んでもない、色彩理論の対象となるものでもない。そんな白に意識を通わせているうちに、ひとつの問いが浮かくせる性質でもない。

び上がってきた。白は単なる色ではなく、むしろ「意匠」あるいは表現の「コンヤプト」として機能しているのではないかという問いである。

情報と生命の原像

　世界は色彩の饗宴である。木々の瑞々しさや水面のきらめき、果実の凝縮感に満ちた色合いやめらめらと燃え上がるたき火の色など、僕らはそのひとつひとつをいとしいと思う。しかし無数の営み、無数のときめきは移ろう時間の中で混ぜあわされ、大きな時間の中では褐色へと流転する。めくるめく自然は色のせめぎあいであり、まるで印象派の画家のパレットのようにひとたび混ぜあわされると、生気に満ちていた個性の饗宴はたちどころにグレーの混沌へと変転するのである。芽吹いた若葉がやがて紅葉し、ついには枯れ葉になるように、まさに「土に帰る」という比喩のごとく。しかし混沌は死ではない。そこにはめくるめく色彩のエネルギーが保存されて胎動し、その中から再びまっさらな色が生まれてくるのである。

　そんな生成と流転のイメージの中に白を置いてみる。白は混沌の中から立ち上ってくる最も鮮烈なイメージの特異点である。混じりあうという負の原理を逆行し、グレーに回帰しようとする退行の引力を突破して表出する。白は特異性の極まりと

して発生するのだ。それはなんの混合でもなく、色ですらない。

エントロピーという概念がある。熱力学の第二法則の中で語られているこの概念は、混沌の度合いを示している。熱力学の第二法則とは、あらゆるエネルギーは平均化されていく方向で保存されるという物理法則である。手の中のコーヒーカップのコーヒーは今、熱く湯気をたてているが、やがてそれは冷めて周辺の温度と同じになってしまう。コーヒーは手に持っているままでは決して熱くなったり、凍ったりはしない。それは確実に冷めていく。しかしコーヒーの熱は失われたわけではなく、周辺の温度と平均化されることで保存されていくのである。東京の気温、シベリアの気温、コンゴ盆地の気温は、生命のような地球の活動のおかげでそれぞれ異なるが、巨大なスケールの時間の中では、やがて同じ温度になっていく。地球の温度も、いつかは周辺宇宙と入り交じって宇宙の果てへと帰趨することを意味している。エントロピーの増加とは、特異性を減じて平均の果てには巨大なエネルギーの混沌世界がある。コーヒーカップの熱も、東京の気温も、地球の温度も、全ての熱エネルギーはひとつの巨大な平均として保存されていく。ただ、この混沌は、死でも無でもない。何ものでもなくなったエネルギーは、同時に何ものにでもなりうる保存された可能性そのものであり、その大いなる無限の混沌から、エントロピー

を減じながら突出してくるものこそ「生」であり「情報」ではないか。エントロピーの引力圏をふりきって飛翔することが生命である。混沌の無意味から屹立してくるものが意味であり情報である。その視点において生命は情報と同義である。

白は、混沌の中から発生する生命あるいは情報の原像である。白はあらゆる混沌から潔癖にのがれきろうとする負のエントロピーの極みである。生命は色として輝くが、白は色をものがれて純粋に混沌の対極に達しようとする志向そのものである。生命は白をまといながら生まれてくるが、具象的な生命は地に足のついた瞬間から色を帯びている。卵から黄色いヒナという生命が現れるように。白は現実の世界で実現されるものではない。僕らは白を見、白に触れたように感じているかもしれないが、それは錯覚である。現実世界の白は必ず汚れている。それは白を目指した痕跡としての存在でしかない。白は繊細で壊れやすい。それは誕生の瞬間ですら完璧な白ではなく、触れるとすぐにそうとは感じられない程度に汚れている。しかし、そうであればこそ白は意識の中にくっきりと屹立する。

象形文字研究の第一人者、白川静博士によると、「白」という漢字は頭蓋骨の象形文字であるという。象形文字が発明された時代に人の心をとらえる白の印象は、野に放置され、風雨や陽光にさらされ漂白された頭蓋骨であったという。その忽然たる白骨の印象は痛いほど明確にイメージできる。砂漠を歩けば獣の骨が、海辺を歩

けば貝殻が点々と砂の上に発見できたであろうが、これらは生の痕跡としての白の印象である。

白は生命の周辺にある。骨は死に接した白であるが、生に接する「乳」や「卵」も白い。授乳は動物にとって重要な営みであり、親の生命を子に渡していくような行為である。この乳が動物も人間も共通して白い。その中には命を育む豊富な滋養が含まれているわけで、僕らが「乳白」と呼ぶ時の白には混濁した有機物のイメージがある。乳の味は「乳白」の味であり有機物の味である。乳首からしたたり落ちる生命の糧が白いということは実に興味深い。

卵もその多くは白い。白い鳥の卵が白いのではなく、青い鳥の卵も、黒い鳥の卵も、さらにはワニの卵も蛇の卵もほの白い。その白の中に現実の生命が宿り、それがあの世とこの世の境界としての皮膜である卵の殻を割って出てきた時には、もはや白ではなく動物の色をしている。生命としてこの世に誕生した動物は既にカオスに向かって歩み始めているということだろうか。

白は大いなる混沌から突出してきた情報すなわち生命のイメージの際にある。混沌は「地」、白は「図」である。地から図を生み出す営みが創造ではないか。混沌たるグレーから白が立ち上がってくるイマジネーションに、世界生成の原像が重なって見えるのである。

第二章

紙

いとしろしき触発力

紙は白い。これはごく当たり前のことのようだが、紙が白いということは決して普通のことではない。白い紙の発明は人類史の中でもひときわ強い光を放つ出来事であったと想像される。紙は今日あまりにも日常的に存在しているので、僕らはその特別さにすっかり慣れてしまっている。しかしながら、前の章でも述べた通り、暮らしの中で白は希少で特別なものであった。その特殊な性質を持った物質を、張りのある薄い枚葉として生み出すことができたわけであるから、紙の誕生が人間にもたらしたイマジネーションにははかりしれないものがあるはずだ。紙の発明は一般的には「書写材」の発明と言われているが、単に「実用」の観点から見るのではなく、白い枚葉の誕生が覚醒させた「イマジネーション」をこそ問題にすべきではないか。確かに紙はメディアである。しかしメディアの本質は実用性のみならず、むしろそれが人間の創造性やコミュニケーションへの衝動をいかに刺激し鼓舞するかという点にある。

紙は、混沌から立ち上がってくる「いとしろしき」ものが物質化したものである。それは褐色の混濁からすくい集められた清浄さの極まりであり、この世に出現した顕在性と可能性のかたまりである。それを目の前にした人類はその未発の可能性に触発され、何かをその上に表現したくてたまらなくなったはずだ。

白い枚葉として

紙は西洋紀元の前後に中国で発明された。後漢の蔡倫（さいりん）がその製法を体系化したとされる。はじめはぼろ布を水の中で突き砕いてばらばらの繊維にしたものを漉き簀（す）で掬い上げて紙にしていたらしい。やがて紙は樹皮の繊維をそのまま叩きほぐして水中に分散させて漉かれるようになった。ベージュの樹皮から純白の紙が生まれてくる。樹皮はアースカラーであるが、必要な繊維だけを残して薄く漉きあげると真っ白な枚葉になる。紙には他の物質にはない独特の張り、そして指先に心地よい肌理（きめ）が備わっている。誤解を恐れずに言えば、もし紙が若葉のような緑色や、熟したような柿色をしていたならば、あるいはビニールのように張りのない触感であったならば、文字や印刷を介在させた文化が、紙の誕生を機にこのように急速には進展してこなかったかもしれない。しかしながら紙は偶然にも色としての属性を持たず、

輝くような「白さ」と、ぴんとした「張り」をたずさえて人類史上に現れた。白には、ことが始まる前の無垢な静謐さや、膨大な成就を呼び込む未発のときめきがたたえられている。一方で、薄く均一な素材は壊れやすくはかなげである。そのような白い紙に墨の黒色で文字や図を置く。その劇的なる対比。ここに人類史上最も重要な感覚の覚醒があったはずだ。文化史の中でひときわまばゆい光を放つイメージの特異点がここにある。

今日、電子メディアの進展によって紙の役割が変わりつつある。「グーテンベルク銀河の終焉」などという言葉も聞こえてくる。紙と印刷技術との相乗効果で生み出されたコミュニケーションの世界は、ひとつの宇宙の爆発的な誕生になぞらえられるわけだが、今日その銀河の命脈も残りいくばくかということか。その比喩は面白いと思うが、紙をメディアと考えてその終焉を評する発想は、紙という物質の意味を少し狭くとらえ過ぎてはいないだろうか。紙は書写・印刷材料である以上に、生命や情報の原像としての「白」を象徴している点で、人類の発想を触発し続けてきた知の触媒である。もしも電子技術を手にした後に紙が発明されたとしても、感覚を意欲させ、創造性をあおる白い枚葉を手にして、おそらく人類はそこでも大きなイマジネーションを得たに違いない。

創造意欲をかき立てる媒質

紙は印刷メディアであると言われる。電子メディアの登場によって、紙はことさらこう呼ばれるようになったが、媒質を持たないことが特徴である電子メディアと違って、紙には「メディア」という概念では言及できない性質があり、そこに紙の本質がある。

文化や文明を少し感覚的な視点で観察すると、その時代に常に人間の近くにあり感覚を覚醒させ、創造への意欲をかきたてた媒質というものが見つかる。たとえば石器時代の石斧(せきふ)などを実際に手で握ってみるとそれが腑に落ちる。石という物質の触り心地や重量感、そして程よい加工適性が人類をその気にさせたのだ。石器時代は驚くほど長い。ひとつの石斧の形が百万年にもわたって伝承されたという。数千世代にもわたって、ひとつの道具の形が継承されるような時間や営みを現代人がイメージすることは難しい。しかし石器という物体の重さと硬さ、持ち心地やテクスチャーが、人類の感覚を鼓舞し、石器文化というものをドライヴさせていく原動力になったことは、それに触れることで直感的に理解できる。今日においてすら、僕は石器を手にしてときめきを覚えた。そのときめきは人間を創造の営みに駆り立てる衝動のようなものだ。

鉄の時代においても同様の洞察が可能だろう。鉄という硬くしなやかで加工性に富んだ媒質が、感覚的に農耕や戦争という能動性を鼓舞したのではなかろうか。鋤（すき）や鍬（くわ）を地面に振り落とし、その先端が土に突き刺さる感触は、土地を開墾し、荒涼たる大地に人為による安らかなる場所を拓いていく意欲を誘ったはずであり、また白い鋼を研磨することで生まれる鋭利な刃というものの質感が、侵略への野望や生死に関わる独特の意識を人の心に宿らせたはずである。

バビロニアの時代には楔形文字（くさびがた）を刻んだ粘土板という媒質がある。粘土板というものは、必ずしも真っ平らな平面ではない。その多くははちきれそうに膨らんでいる。表面にはびっしりと細やかな楔形文字が刻み付けられている。なぜ、粘土板がこんなにも膨らんで反り返っているのか。

おそらくは、手で持てる携帯可能な物体に、より多くの表面積をもたらせるためにそうなったのではないかと想像される。つまり、粘土板にコンパクトに文字を刻み付けるという強い意欲が、より小さな文字の刻印、そして少しでも多い表面を生み出す心性を育み、粘土板の膨らみを生み出したのではないか。文字を彫りつけられたこの固体から、そういう意欲のほとばしりを読み解くことができる。文化は人間の意欲に呼応している。意欲という帆をはちきれんばかりに膨らませる風の一翼を担うもの。そういう物質が、文化や文明の傍らには必ずある。

紙もまた、その白さと張りによって、人類の意欲をそそり続けてきたのである。紙の白さは単に文字や写真をのせるための無機質でニュートラルな平面ではない。紙の白やその物質性と感覚的に対話を続けることで、人間はそこに肥沃な表現の領域を育むことができた。書籍はそのようなものとして文化の中に立ち上がってきた道具である。今日、電子メディアの意味を考え、掘り下げる上でも、空気のように自分たちの日常に寄り添い、そこに力を与え続けてきた媒介物の意味を、感覚を通して評価し直す必要があるのではないだろうか。

反芻する白

僕の仕事はモニターの前でキーボードに触れている時間が少なくない。こうして文章を書くにもキーボードを叩いている。しかし紙に触れる時間も同じくらいある。そのときは、脳の別の場所が目覚めてくる感触があり、脳の消費エネルギーがぐっと増える気がする。ペンや鉛筆の先で、紙に触れる場合もそうだが、特に印刷用紙を選ぶとか、書籍の造本用紙を検討するときなどは、目や指先を通してまさに感覚の産毛をさかだてながら白い紙を触っている。触るというよりも白を反芻するといった方がふさわしいかもしれない。反芻とは牛などが一度呑み込んだ牧草をもう一度

戻して咀嚼することであるが、自分の場合はイメージの反芻である。記憶の中におびただしく堆積している白を呼び出して、目の前にある白い紙と対照させながら吟味する。その感覚は選ぶとか検討するというよりも、やはり反芻するといった方がぴったりくる。

　書籍のデザインは、白い紙の組み合わせから始まる。表紙やカバー、見返しや化粧扉、そして本文用紙の質をそれぞれに吟味していく。近年、紙は着色されていないものを用いる場合が多い。なぜ色のついた紙ではなく、白い紙にことさら注目するようになったのだろうか。かつては、色のついた紙に熱中し、紙見本帖のバラエティの豊富さを片端から堪能していたはずが、いつの間にか白い紙ばかりを選んでいる。デザインとは差異のコントロールだが、仕事を無数に繰り返すうちに、本当に必要な差異だけでいいと思うようになった。大きな段差は必要ではなく、最小の差異のみで意味の編み物を編みたいと思うようになった。その方がずっとデリケートな編み物になる。特に巷に色が溢れ、紙でもパソコンでも何百何千という色が自在に使えるようになればなるほど、色彩の多様性に魅力を感じなくなった。切実な材料だけを俎上に置く。そう思い続けてデザインをしていたかもしれない。そうするうちに、色はいつの間にか冗長なもの、余分な要素になっていったのである。もちろん、伝統色の例でお話しした通り、色は文化そのものである。モノクロー

ムの写真は美しいが、世界から色彩が消えてしまったら、モノクロームの意味すらも消える。人工色が醜いと言うつもりもない。むしろ原色やヴィヴィッドな色彩をふんだんに謳歌できる才能にはあこがれすら感じる。現実感のない仮想世界で純粋に色彩を操作できるカラー・コンピューティングの世界にも魅力を感じる。そしてもちろん、普段のデザインで色を用いないわけではない。僕は白の好きなデザイナーでもなければ、色を使わないデザイナーでもない。プロのグラフィックデザイナーであるから色は当然用いる。ただし色を用いる場合ははっきりと明快な「機能性」を意識しているかもしれない。つまり消火器の色や緊急ボタンの色は赤がふさわしいと考えるし、サインシステムの色彩は環境から浮かび上がる色彩を選択するだろう。

しかしながら、情緒や細やかな感覚の差異に目を凝らしているうちに、気がつくと人工的な色彩の氾濫をのがれて、天然自然のさりげない色を志向している。明るくヴィヴィッドな主張よりも、古い書物の風化した紙の色彩や、古紙の混入したボール紙のグレー、あるいは鉄錆のあやうい発色にときめきを感じ、植物の種や、砂の色といったシックで自然な色にリアリティや共感を覚えるのである。その中でも特に魅力を感じ、様々な印象を刻んできたものが「白」である。

白い紙は無数にある。表面が鏡のようにつるつるしたものから、鮫肌のような荒

白｜紙

い肌のもの、石膏のように平滑で無光沢のもの、卵の殻のような手触りを持つもの、雲母の入ったきらら光沢を持つもの、雪のように白いもの、曇り空のように曖昧なもの、生成りの風合いを持つもの、柔らかいもの、腰の強いしなやかなもの、平板で硬質なもの、絨毯のように分厚いもの、宙に浮遊するほど薄いものなどなど……。それこそ際限なくある。書籍用紙の選定作業は、所詮白の組み合わせであるから、短時間で終わるだろうと自分でも考えがちだが、いつもおびただしい白を目の前に広げては思いのほか苦しい時間を過ごしている。赤い白、青い白、黄色い白のバランスを調整し、繊維の長さや厚みなど、それぞれの性質を吟味していくことで、カバーはより強い沈黙をたたえ、見返しは初めて開かれたような初々しさを、化粧扉は何かのはじまりを告げる節目の質感を伝え、そして本文は文字や写真を際立たせる背景として、あるいは指先に書物の触り心地をささやく肌理として、それぞれの役回りの中に次第に落ち着いていくのである。

白は隣の色との相関の中で浮き沈みする。対比において輝きを増したり、背景に後退したり、くすんだりする。今日、紙は工業製品であり、そこには白さを計測する基準がある。物理的に白い色が必ずしも最も白い印象を呼び起こすわけではない。測定値としての白の基準のひとつは炭酸マグネシウムという物質である。鉄棒の演技をする体操選手が演技の前に白い粉を手につけているシーンを時折目にするが、

あれが炭酸マグネシウムである。この粉の白色度が白さの基準になっている。炭酸マグネシウムに比べてどのくらい白くないかが紙の白さの度合いとして示されてきた。最近ではその炭酸マグネシウムよりも、もう少し白い紙が開発された。それも蛍光インクを用いたような青白さではなく、純白の白。この紙の白さは傑出していて、他の紙と並べると歴然と白い。だから白を強調したい場合にはこの紙を用いることもある。

　しかしあるときに気が付いた。白色度の高い紙を用いただけでは白さを印象づけることができない。表紙や帯、見返しや本文用紙のそれぞれにていねいに気が配られている書籍と比べると、白いだけの本は白の力が弱い。人間の目は暗さにも白さにもすぐに順応するせいか、白色度だけでは白の印象が軽いのだ。むしろ透明感や不透明感、重みや軽さが吟味され、それらが共鳴して白のオーケストレーションが達成されているようなものに、より強い印象として白が感じられる。卵の殻のような肌合いを持つ表紙を半透明のグラシン紙で覆うことで秘せられた奥行きの白が生まれる。あるいは鏡のような半滑な白をめくる中に漆喰のような無光沢の白が現れると、そこにはっと荘厳な光が満ちる。

　白色度というのは物理的な指標であって感受性の指標ではない。したがって白色度が高いというだけでは白は印象づけられないのである。咲き乱れる花々の印象は

真っ白でも、その背後にコピー用紙程度の紙を置いてみると、花そのものの白さは紙の白さほどではないことに気が付く。花弁は淡い色を含み水分をたたえた重たい白である。しかし咲き誇る花々が僕らの心に届けてくる白は鮮烈に白い。要するに白は感覚の中に湧き起こる現象なのだ。

それらの白を目と指先、そして記憶を動員しながら反芻し、反芻し、反芻して本の基礎が出来上がってゆく。本をデザインする場合には、印刷されていない白い本を試作する。これを「束見本（つかみほん）」と呼ぶ。束見本は言わば紙でできたイメージの建築である。この白い建築を僕は無数に建ててきた。情報は白い花のごとくあれと無意識のうちに考えているのかもしれない。デザイナーとしての自分の感覚の背景のひとつはここにあるのだと思う。

　　白い四角い紙

　白い四角
　のなか
　の白い四角
　のなか

の白い四角
のなか
の白い四角
のなか
の白い四角

　これは北園克衛(きたそのかつえ)の詩「単調な空間」の部分であるが、この詩に触発されて生まれてくるイメージは随分と白い。ひとつ前の白い四角よりも、新しい白い四角の方がより白く感じる。その四角の中に生まれる次の四角はもっと白く感じる。一連の白はとても観念的な白であると言えるが、白が感受性であるとするならここに示された白はその本質に接近していくものである。さらに言えば、白が四角として表現されていることも、白さを一層際立たせているように感じる。そのせいか、これは具象的なイメージとしての紙漉きの営みをも彷彿させる。白い紙料液の中からより白い紙が次々と掬い上げられてくる。既に出来上がった紙よりも、たった今出来上がった紙の方がより白く感じられる。その反復で白が延々と生産され続けていく。まるで生命を生み出すはずみ車が回っているような、そういうイメージを汲み取ることのできる詩である。

白｜紙

言葉を畳む

書籍は、人間の叡智として生産された言葉を貯蔵する場所として、誕生以来多くの工夫が加えられてきた。また、書物の中に文字をおさめる文字制御の作法は、書物に格納されるべきものとして峻別されたテキストを、書籍の中に座らせるための知恵、技術、あるいは美意識や思想として発達してきた。

紙が発明される以前、ヨーロッパから中近東では、羊の皮をなめしたベラムやパーチメントと呼ばれる薄様の皮革が書写材として用いられた。古くエジプトではパピルスという植物の茎を、縦方向にスライスして重ね、プレスし、乾かしてシート状にしたものが用いられた。中国では木簡や竹簡といって、竹や木を薄い短冊状にしたものを紐で連結させ、そこに文字を書いた。いずれの書写材も四角い形に仕上げられている。羊の皮はそのままなめすと、平らにしても羊の体の形をしているはずだが、文字や記号が記されたものはどれも四角い。楔形文字が刻まれている粘土板も上から見ると四角い。人間は自然を四角くしつらえ直すことで自らの環境を作ってきた。

自然の中には四角いものは案外と少ない。ある鉱物の結晶は完全な立方体に近いが、むしろ稀な例と言える。自然のうちに数理が潜んでいることは近代科学の成果

の通りであるから、四角を形成する数理が自然の中にあることに不思議はない。ただし構造体としての四角は非常に不安定であるために、その姿が自然には発現しにくいのだ。しかし、人類は四角が好きである。二本の手を持つ人間が、大きな木の葉のようなものを二つに折ると、それをもうひとつ折ると、紐や蔓が重力の方向に垂直に垂れ下がることから垂直を認識し、それが四角の端緒になったかは分からない。この話をつきつめると果てしなくイメージが広がりそうであるが、ともかくも羊の形をしたシートは四角く裁断されて書写材になった。有機的な形を四角く断つことはデザインの発端のひとつかもしれない。

ちなみに工業製品として生産される現代の紙は細長いロール状に巻き上げられて生まれてくる。これが $1:\sqrt{2}$ という比率で裁断されて枚葉の紙となる。$1:\sqrt{2}$ という比率は、半分に折っても、そのまた半分に折っても、縦と横の比率が変わらない。テレビやコンピュータのモニター画面も四角いが、折る必要性のないモニターは人間の目が横に二つ並んでついていることを反映してか、視野に比例して横長に進化してきた。

書籍は四角い紙でできている。この四角いスペースの中に、言葉をどう折り畳んで収納するか。基本的に言葉は時間に沿った一本の線のように連続的な構造を持つ

ている。人間は三重奏のようには言葉を発することができない。そんなことができなければコミュニケーションは随分と複雑になるだろうが、現在までの人間の発声能力においてこの言葉はソロ楽器のように単線で発せられる。言葉を文字に置き換えていく際にもこの一本の連続的な構造は変わらない。したがって、限られたスペースに紐のように線的な言葉を折り畳んでおさめることが、書籍という器の仕組みである。

ヨーロッパ系の文字は左から右に横書きで、漢字圏の文字は上から下に縦書きに文字を配している。行・草書やスクリプト系の表記を除外して考えるならば、象形文字であろうと、表音文字であろうと、文字は元来アトミックな部品を線的に配列するという発想から生み出されたものであるから、右から並べようと、左から並べようと、さらには下から上に並べようと自由である。アルファベットの祖先にあたる紀元前のフェニキア文字は当初は右から左へ配されていたが、そのうちに牛耕式といって、右から左へ、さらに左から右へと、牛が田畑を耕す軌跡のように文字を描く方法へと移行し、その後に左から右へ行って改行する形式に定着したようである。

木簡や竹簡に記す場合も、羊皮紙に書く場合も、主に右手で筆記具を持って連続して文字を記していく習慣からくる合理性か、左から右、あるいは上から下という文字を折り畳む方向が自然と決まってきた。今日では漢字文化圏ですら、左から右の横書きが徐々に主流を占めつつあるが、書物が文字を格納するメディアであると

いう観点で言うと、合理性と効率によって次第にその趨勢が決められていくのであろう。

文字というもの

一方で、文字というものがいかなる有様としてどんな土台の上に座るかという観点、すなわち文字を書籍というオブジェクトにしつらえていく際の美意識が、合理性とは異なる動機から生まれてきている。ひとつひとつの文字は言語でありながら、同時にそれは美的なイメージを担う造形物でもあった。

ローマ時代のアルファベットは石に彫刻されることが多かったために、ローマン系の書体は刃物で文字の端を整えるセリフという突起を持つ。つまり目に見え形質として発現したとたんに、文字は美を意識する心によってその形を整えられてきた。記された言葉は政治や宗教などの力と常に密接な関係にあったために、文字やその集積はある種のオーラを発するような精緻な構築物へとおのずと向かっていく。つまり読めればいいというものではなく、立派に、荘厳に、格式を持って存在することが運命づけられていた。『マグナカルタ』（大憲章）を羊皮紙に記したマニュスクリプトの集積などは思わずひれ伏してしまいそうな威圧感があるが、これはテキ

ストの権威を文字群として表象させるという、高密度に配された手書き文字の「威」を意識して制作されたはずである。

漢字文化圏では詩や教典、禅語などを表記する「書」という営みに高度な奥行きが生まれ、発話される言語とは異なる文字表現の世界が、紙の白と墨の黒の相克によって絶妙な成熟を遂げていく。中国では筆という筆記具が比較的早く成熟したと見え、石に彫られた文字にも筆の造形の痕跡がはっきりとある。すなわち文字を顕現させるという行為は、言語行為を超えてどんどん目的化されていったわけである。

もちろん、ひれ伏したくなるような威丈高な傾向だけが文字ではなく、むしろその威を解きほぐしてやさしくやわらかく人間の心情の機微に添うような文字の表情を志向する動きもある。平安時代に日本で発案されたひらがなは、威丈高で教養主義的な漢字を、しなやかに解体するような美意識が背景にある。平安時代の日本にはもっぱら女性がこのひらがなを駆使して文学の領域で活動するようになる。ひらがなは権威主義的なるものよりもむしろ、繊細な情緒や心の機微を表記すべく、白い和紙の上にたゆたうように文字を踊らせるように記された。このような文字表現もまた、言語的なるものを超えた文字の美意識のなせる技なのである。

さて、このような事例を、洋の東西を横断して次々に列挙することが本書の目的ではない。四角い平面の中で、文字は言語的な意味を超えた「造形物」としての美

を成熟させてきたことを確認したい。いとしろしく張りのある四角い紙の発明は、その美意識を悠々と跳躍させる要因となったはずである。叡智は紙にいざなわれて次々と生まれ出た。やがて叡智を記録する文字というものの周辺に美意識が育まれ、紙はさらなる知恵と美の生産と蓄積を担う媒体として進化していったのである。そのような営みの中に中世という果てしない時間が織りなされていったことを、僕らは今日、少しばかりのエネルギーを費やして想像してみるべきではないだろうか。

活字とタイポグラフィ

活版印刷術の発明は情報の複製と流通における大きな革命であったが、一方でそれは紙の上に文字を配する新たな美学の幕開けでもあった。グーテンベルクが活版印刷を始めた際、その主な目的は聖書の印刷であったが、そこに用いられた活字は、今日電子メディアの中を飛び交っている合理的な視覚言語としての文字ではなく、紙の上に忽然とインクで屹立する様式隆々たるゴシック書体であった。「インキュナブラ」と呼ばれる初期のグーテンベルク本は、手書きの写本に負けない威信と品格を示そうと、相当に気張っていたわけであるが、そこには、手書き文字の代用品ではなく「活字」という、規格性、反復性が生み出す新しい文字造形のモチベーショ

ンが潜んでいた。紙に黒々と食いつく活字の刷り上がりは、手で書く文字とは異なる味わいの印字面と手触りを白い紙の上に発現させていたはずで、何事にも美を見出そうとする人類が、組版活字に潜在する美を見過ごすはずもなく、以後、無数の活字設計者たちによってそこにおびただしい情熱が注がれることになる。タイポグラフィとはそのような情熱を発露する領域のことを言う。

アルファベットを例にとると、汎用性・可読性に優れた「ローマン体」活字を設計したニコラス・ジェンセンや、携帯できる実用書籍に貢献する「イタリック」書体を設計したアルドゥス・マヌティウスなど、十五世紀後半のヴェネツィアを中心とするイタリアがまずタイポグラフィの洗練に先鞭をつけた。活字の設計は、知性と造形感覚の程よい均衡が必要な仕事であり、文化と技術とのせめぎあいの中、その後のヨーロッパで無数の試行錯誤を経て磨かれていくのである。

やがて近代の芸術運動の中に、タイポグラフィも巻き込まれていく。過去の様式が一度完全に解体・再構築される波に文字も巻き込まれ、ローマン体の特徴であるセリフはそのうねりの中で削り取られていく。いわゆるサンセリフ（セリフのない）書体の登場である。モダンタイポグラフィの飛躍を決定づけたサンセリフの傑作「ヘルベチカ」を設計したマックス・ミーディンガーや、活字のウエイトや縦横比の変化を総合的な書体ファミリーに集約した「ユニバース」のアドリアン・フルティガー

など、二十世紀中葉のスイスがモダン・タイプフェイスのエポックを独占する優れた仕事をした。書体の充実と同時に、文字の統辞法そのものも洗練され、同じくスイスのタイポグラフィが近代タイポグラフィの基礎を築いていくのもこの頃である。
　このように時代や思想、印刷を巡る技術や考え方は違えども、書籍と文字に向き合う美意識と情熱は、こつこつとたゆみなく書籍の歴史を作ってきたのである。
　一方、中国ではグーテンベルクにさかのぼること四百年ほど前の十一世紀、宋の時代に既に美しい楷書体の陶製活字が畢昇という技術者によって制作されている。当時の中国では木の版木にページごと文字を彫刻する木版印刷が実用化されており、陶製の活字はその効率化をねらったもののようだ。しかし、数千から数万の単位に及ぶ文字の数が、中国の活字のシステムには進化させなかった。さらに言えば、金属や陶製の印刷文字の品質が木版印刷の仕上がり精度に比べて劣っていたという美的な視点が、中国鋳造活字の進化を遅らせた理由のひとつであったと考えられる。
　中国の場合、文字の規範に見える「楷書」の誕生は行書や草書よりも遅い。つまり、楷書が崩されて行書や草書が生まれたわけではない。最も古い書体は秦の始皇帝が定めた小篆（しょうてん）と呼ばれる篆書（てんしょ）と隷書（れいしょ）である。一点・一画の造形よりも文字全体の象形性の方が重視された漢字であるが、時代が下るにしたがい、筆によって育まれた細部の形が整理され、やがては欧陽詢（おうようじゅん）という卓越した能書家の出現によって「楷書」

白｜紙

という規範が確立されてくる。八世紀、唐代のことである。宋代の陶製活字や木版の原形となるのがこの楷書である。

木版に楷書を彫る彫刻的な造形が生み出した書体は「宋朝体」と呼ばれるもので、漢字活字の歴史に一石を投じる優美な書体であったが、時代を経るうちに宋朝体はさらに抽象の度を増し、清代の『康熙字典』による文字の規格化を経て今日の「明朝体」へと推移していく。

今日漢字文化圏で用いられている明朝体には「ウロコ」という末端の造作がある。これは楷書の起筆、終筆の反映であるが、白い紙に映える活字の可読性と造形性の双方から洗練を加えられてこうなったと考えられる。

活版印刷技術としての鋳造活字が中国で用いられるようになるのは、清代の末期に東アジアで活動した西洋のキリスト教の活版印刷術との交流を経てである。今日

I

ローマン体
Garamond Regular

一

明朝体
リュウミン H-KL

おびただしい歳月を経て
文字はこのような形に
到達した。

の明朝体が欧文書体ボドニーなどとの類似性を持つのは、ローマン体を鋳造していた西洋の活版印刷術が、布教のために当時の中国の明朝体を解釈・鋳造し、それが活版印刷のシステムごと中国に流入された経緯によるものと推察される。日本における鋳造活字のルーツもここにある。

洋の東西を問わず、彫刻あるいは鋳造された文字が紙に刷り取られて書物が出来上がるというプロセスの中で、紙上に文字を座らせる作法を通して、活字の美意識が大きく開花していった。その点は、グーテンベルクも中国の版木も同じである。文字は白との対比の中で、紙の上に黒々と刻印されるオブジェクトとして独自の美を発展させていくことになる。

ゴシック様式として始まったアルファベット活字、あるいは楷書を基本とする中国活字は、歴史の中で、読みやすさというフィルターで濾過され、見飽きない普遍性という視線にさらされ続けることで洗練の度を加えてきたのである。甲骨に文字を刻みはじめてのち、紙に黒々とウロコを屹立させる明朝体が完成するまで、あるいは、大理石にノミでオールドローマンの文字が刻印されて以来、その優美な曲線が「ユニバース」の均整のとれた曲線に集約されるまでに、実に気の遠くなるような工夫と実践の歴史が介在している。

その膨大なイメージの厚みを通過して、文字は今、紙の上に座っている。

白　｜　紙

第三章

空白　エンプティネス

空白の意味

白は時に「空白」を意味する。色彩の不在としての白の概念は、そのまま不在性そのものの象徴へと発展する。しかしこの空白は、「無」や「エネルギーの不在」ではなく、むしろ未来に充実した中身が満たされるべき「機前の可能性」として示される場合が多く、そのような白の運用はコミュニケーションに強い力を生み出す。空っぽの器には何も入っていないが、これを無価値と見ず、何かが入る「予兆」と見立てる創造性がエンプティネスに力を与える。このような「空白」あるいは「エンプティネス」のコミュニケーションにおける力と、白は強く結びついている。

長谷川等伯　松林図屏風

日本美術の中で、最も人気のある作品のひとつに、長谷川等伯の「松林図」がある。

これは六曲一雙すなわち六枚つながりの画面が左右一対に配された屏風である。勢

いのある筆触で松林が描かれているが、この作品の中には様々な白や空白が運用されている。

第一には、松の木そのものが荒い筆遣いで描かれており、必ずしも緻密な写実性を持たないこの筆致によって僕らはむしろリアルな松を想起させられてしまう。ラフな筆触の荒削りな刺激に触発されて、記憶の引き出しから、松林の詳細な風情が誘い出されるようだ。松林図はモノトーンの荒漠とした絵画である。

この水墨画は、中国絵画の精華、南宋の水墨画の遺産を引き継いでいる。水墨画は宋の時代にひとつの頂点を迎え、その成果は西洋におけるルネサンス期の絵画に匹敵する。精緻を極めた描法で世界や宇宙の摂理を表象するかのような北宋画、そして「精緻」と「朦朧」を交錯させ、もののリアリティや構造の再現ではなく、茫洋とした余白、すなわちイメージの解放区を紙面に展開したのが南宋画。宋代の水墨画はこのふたつに大別される。おそらくは南宋の画家、牧谿の絵に等伯はどこかで接したはずである。余白／空白は、等伯の松林図においてはっきりと主題として開花し、絶妙に結晶している。精緻な描き込みを意図的に回避することで、逆に見る側のイメージを活性化させ、描かれていない部分に、見る側の活発なイメージの生成を呼び起こす。結果として大きなイマジネーションを覚醒させるのである。つまり、表現の粗さと省略が豊富なイマジネーションを覚醒させるのである。

白 ｜ 空白　エンプティネス

水墨画には破墨と呼ばれるものがある。破墨とは荒く素早い筆法、すなわち精緻な描写からの逸脱を意味する。リアルな描写をのがれた粗の筆致、それゆえに、見る側がその未発の景観を補完し、イメージのほとばしりを加速させる。そのような仕組みを言う。同じ仕組みが松林図には備わっている。

さらに、この絵は、松の木を描いているというよりも、松の木々の間の空間を描いているように見える。画面に描かれた主役は松の木々ではなく、むしろ霞む木々を手がかりに、大気そのものを描いているという感じか。松林が空間の奥に向かうにしたがって朦朧となり、白い空間の中に溶けていく。白い空間は不在としてではなく、その向こうに無数の松を蔵する濃密な奥行きとして意識される。大気は密度と運動をはらんで絶妙な質感に満ち、見る者は、感覚をその白い空間の媒質の中に心地よく漂わせることができるのだ。澱みのある湿潤な余白の中に視線を泳がせていく浮遊感がこの絵の生命であると言ってもいい。

左隻の右上、すなわち一双の画面のまん中左上あたりには、霊峰を思わせる山がひときわ白く描かれており、この白の中の白こそ最も遠い遠景である。そこから手前は、絵画上では空白として描かれているが、逆に言えば、靄の白に隠れているだけで、そこには遠景から近景までの膨大なる景色が埋蔵されていることになる。そのようなイメージを包含しつつ、僕らは松の間の白い空白に感覚をゆだね、たゆた

このような、何もない空白に、細密な描写以上の豊かなイマジネーションを見立てていくという、逆説的な絵画表現を日本人は尊び、育んできた。長谷川等伯の松林図はそのひとつの典型である。「白紙も模様のうちなれば心にてふさぐべし」とは江戸時代の絵画の技法書『本朝画法大伝』に記された言葉である。描かれていない空白地帯を情報のゼロ地帯とは見なさない。それどころか、そこにこそ意味の比重を加算しようとする心性が日本の美意識の重要な一端を作っている。そこに「白」の、コミュニケーションのコンセプトとしての重要な側面がある。

満ちる可能性としての空白

　何もないということは、何かを受け入れることで満たされる可能性を持つということである。空っぽの器を負の意味に取らず、むしろ満ちるべき潜在力と見るところに、コミュニケーションの力学が動き出す。日本の神道は自然の中に八百万（やおよろず）の神を見立てる宗教であるが、別の見方をすると、それはどこからでも神を招き入れ、イメージの力を運用するコミュニケーションの技術でもある。その仕組みを空白に関係づけて説明してみよう。

白　｜　空白　エンプティネス

日本の「神社」という、人々の信仰の営みを受け入れる空間の中枢は、「代」あるいは「屋代」であるが、これは「空白を抱く」という基本原理からなる。地面の上に、四方に柱を立て、それぞれの柱の頭頂部を縄で結ぶ。これが「代」の原形である。

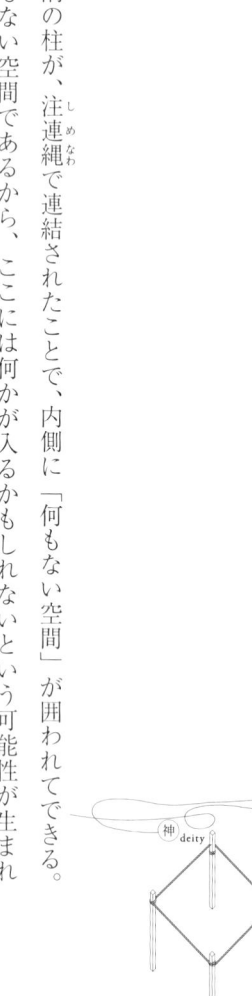

四隅の柱が、注連縄で連結されたことで、内側に「何もない空間」が囲われてできる。何もない空間であるから、ここには何かが入るかもしれないという可能性が生まれる。この「かもしれない」という可能性こそ重要であり、その潜在性に対して手を合わせるという意識の動きが神道の信仰心である。

日本人がイメージした八百万の神は、ひと所に局在する神ではなく、あまねく世界全体に遍在する神である。里の家の上をふわふわと飛んでいたり、海や山の上をゆったりと飛んでいたりする。引っこ抜いた大根の先にいるかと思えば、森の樹々の間に浮かんでいたりする。米粒の間にも七人の神が潜み、掬った水の中にも、腐敗した汚物の中にすら座っている。神々は、自在に世界に遍在するが、これを拉致

して自分たちのために働いてもらうことはかなわない。ただし、意図的に「空白」をしつらえたなら、空白があるゆえに神はそこに入るかもしれない。なぜなら、空白はものが宿る可能性そのものであるから、神はそれを見逃さないはずである。

こうして「代」は神が訪れ入り込む可能性の「寄り代」としてしつらえられ、四つの柱に注連縄の張られた空なる空間が生まれた。漂泊する神「客神」が飛来し宿る「かもしれない」という可能性に手を合わせ、意識を集中させる営み、すなわち神道という日本古来の宗教は、こうして始まったのである。

「屋代」とは屋根のかかった「代」すなわち、中央に空白を宿した屋根付きの空間のことである。この屋代を、内と外を融通させる透過性のある垣を巡らせ、くぐるべき通路を示す鳥居を配して構造化したものが神社である。こうして人々は、神社に参拝する。鳥居をくぐり、屋代にたどり着き、柏手を打ち、屋代の奥に向かって、

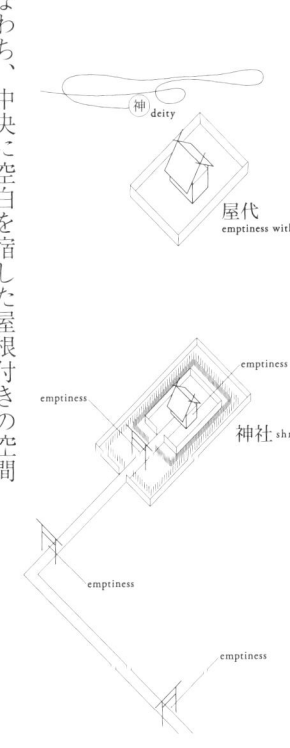

屋 roof
代 emptiness
神 deity
屋代 emptiness with a roof
emptiness
emptiness
神社 shrine
emptiness
emptiness

白 ｜ 空白　エンプティネス

思いを放つ。屋代の基本は空白であるから、そうした人々の思いを受け入れる器としても機能する。空なる中枢は、意味を発信するのではなく、ひたすら人々の思いを受け入れる器に徹することで役割を果たす。賽銭箱という、これも空っぽの箱がそこに配置されており、人々はこの空の箱に思いとともに金銭を投じる。神と人間との媒介である神社は、ひたすらエンプティネスであり続けることで、その役割を果たすのである。人々は、神が宿るかもしれない可能性としての屋代に、自身の思いをも投げ入れて心の安寧を得る。宗教とは、不可知で神秘的なるものと人間との対話である。日本の場合は、このようなエンプティネスを介してその対話がなされていると考えてよい。

伊勢神宮と情報

伊勢神宮のように複雑に見える神社も、基本の構造は同じである。中央に空白を抱えて、それは満たされる潜在性として力を発揮している。白は色の不在であると同時に、空白の象徴でもある。四つの柱を結ぶ注連縄には白い紙で出来た御幣が下げられる。屋代へ通じるアプローチには白い玉砂利が敷きつめられ、神の領域と人の領域の境界は、白布の御帳で仕切られている。時折、風が吹くと、白い布はひら

ひらと風にあおられて、二つの領域の境界に融通が起こる。何かが生きて通っているように感じられるのである。

伊勢神宮の建築は、南方ポリネシア系の建築様式の影響を受けているように見える。日本は、シルクロードを経て遠くローマから伝播された文化を、中国、朝鮮を経由して受け入れたと考えられがちであるが、アジアの端に浮かんでいる島国は、海を介して世界と等しくつながっている。つまり、度合いの差こそあれ、世界中から文化の影響を受けている。伊勢神宮の建築は明らかに太平洋、ポリネシア系の建築的影響を示している。ただし、これを千数百年を超えて、倦まず撓まず咀嚼し工夫を重ねて、純日本的なるものへと変容させてきた。

伊勢神宮は式年造替といって二十年ごとに神社の建築を全て建て替え刷新する。つまり屋代は二十年の寿命しか持たない。そのために、屋代はその脇に更新されるべきもう一つ別のスペースを持っている。したがって、二十年に一度、新旧二つの建築が並列する。内にある千数百点に及ぶ祭具も全て新しくしつらえられて新たな建物へと納められる。そして古い建物は解体され消滅する。

神社建築の図面も二十年に一度描き直される。オリジナル図面を保存するのではなく、描き直して伝承するところが独特である。描き直されることによって物理的差異は当然生じるはずだが、描き直すことこそ精密なる伝承と考える感受性にこそ

白 ｜ 空白　エンプティネス

注目すべきである。写すことで情報は新たな生命を得て更新される。
建築は宮大工の技術の伝承によって受け継がれている。かつて親方を手伝った大工が、後の造替で親方となって仕事を仕切る。新たな屋代の棟上げの際に、大工の棟梁が発する呪言があるが、これは既に言語としての意味をなさず、まさに再現されるべき呪言として口承されているという。

図面の写しや技術の伝承という過程を経て継がれてきた神社建築は、千数百年の歴史の中で、僅かずつオリジナルを逸脱し、日本的な感受性の中で、しかるべき方向へと変容した。ポリネシア風の建築は、きりりと簡素な日本流に変容を遂げたのである。これはDNAの情報を写し更新し続けることで持続し、また進化もする生命の営みとも似ている。

白は混沌から立ち上がってくる情報そのものであり、生命であると、すでに述べたが、造替という営みは、一度建築をカオスへと戻し、そこから新たに、技の伝承という生成装置を経て立ち上げ直していく刷新のプロセスである。あえて混沌をくぐらせることによって、まさに「いとしろしき」情報として神宮を再生させる試みである。これによって手垢のついた「既知なるもの」はまっさらの「未知なるもの」として更新される。檜の白木で構築される新たな屋代はまさに白く神々しい。白い装束をまとった神官たちが神事をとりおこなう営みは、まさに白を巡り、空

白を運用する営みである。これは日本古来の宗教の形であるが、それは同時に、環境形成すなわちデザインの形でもある。日本におけるコミュニケーションの中枢はこのような「空白」であり、その空白は、白という概念とともにある。

何も言わない

コミュニケーションとは、有意味な内容物の受け渡しであると考えられがちであるが、必ずしも内容物を介さなくてもコミュニケーションは成り立つ。コミュニケーションとは人と人の意識が疎通することであり、それは目と目を合わせるアイコンタクトのようなものも含まれる。目を合わせてうなずき合うことは、必ずしも何かを伝達したことにはならないが、双方が意識を通わせ合えたとするならば、それをコミュニケーションと考えて差し支えはない。ある内容を分かりやすい合理的な情報の建築にしつらえて、それをメディアを通して効率良く送り届け、理解し合うような仕組みがコミュニケーションと呼ばれている。しかしコミュニケーションの形は記号のやり取りに終始するばかりではない。結果として互いにうなずき合えればそこに絆は生まれ得る。記号のエンコードやデコードを経て意味を解読し合うような手間を省いて、アイコンタクトをするだけで了解できれば、こんなに効率の良い

白 ｜ 空白　エンプティネス

コミュニケーションはない。日本ではこのような理想的なコミュニケーションが生まれている状況を「阿吽の呼吸」という。神社の入り口の左右に立っている狛犬の片方は「あ」と息を吐き、他方は「うん」と息をのむ。コミュニケーションに喩えれば、何かを発している状態と、受け入れている状態。これが同時に行われて、瞬時の了解が相互に生まれている状況が阿吽の呼吸である。

日本人のコミュニケーションは分かりづらいと批判されることがある。伝えたい事柄を明言せず、ぼかしてしまう。主語をはっきりさせない。だから、全てを明確にし、論理構造を用いて、曖昧なままでことを進めようとする。主体を顕在化させる西洋式のコミュニケーションの文脈では理解しにくいということであろう。しかし、「阿吽の呼吸」や「根回し」「腹芸」は高度なコミュニケーションでもある。主体をはっきりさせなかったり、責任者を特定できなくしたり、言わずもがなでことをすませることは、暗黙裏の合意形成のシステムである。そのようなコンセンサスが自然と共有される事態は、錬度の高い集団的コミュニケーションの結果であり、それ自体は優れた伝達技術であると考えた方が自然である。今日のように、インターネットを介した膨大な集団コミュニケーションが動き出している状況においては、むしろこのような合意形成の手法が精密に読み直され、研究される必要があるだろう。

極めて大事な決定をする時に、決定の対象となるものやことを直接指示せず、それを括弧にくるんで扱うという方法は、空白のコミュニケーションであり、エンプティネスの運用である。

「あれ（　）はそういうこと（　）でよろしいでしょうか」

一同無言。

「ご異議がございませんようですので、あれ（　）はそういうこと（　）ですすめさせていただきます」

などという局面を理解できない外国人がいたならば、切実なる主題を直接的な名詞で言明する荒々しさを避け、代名詞で行うという抑制の効かせ方と、誰かが決めたのではなく、そこに居合わせた全ての人々が、空の器に盛られ、代名詞化されて示された主題の行方を黙認することで、参加者全員が等しくその決定事項の責任を分担するというコミュニケーションのメカニズムを説明してあげなくてはいけない。曖昧さを残し、いい加減にものごとを決めているのではなく、当事者だけが理解できる方法で精密にエンプティネスを運用し、合意を形成し、責任や権力の偏在を回避しているのである。中枢は埋めるのではなくあえて空白にしておくことで融通を

持たせ、潤滑な合意を生み出す仕組みがここにはある。ずるがしこい政治家がこの仕組みを悪用して責任を回避する構図が時にクローズアップされるので、このコミュニケーションの仕組みそのものがいかがわしく見えてしまう傾向があるが、本質はそうではない。

交差点を十文字に交差させてしまうと、そこには必ず信号機を設置して、「行け」と「止まれ」を峻別する必要が生じる。しかしながら、丸い円を交差点に配した「ラウンダーバード」という仕組みを用いるならば、全てのクルマを停止することなく、進みたい方向に進んでいくことができる。もちろんこの比喩は正確ではないが、意味の中央をエンプティにすることは、十文字の交差点のような特異点を、コミュニケーションの俎上から巧妙に外していく技術なのである。大事な中枢を括弧でくくって中央を空白にすることで、時にそこに入るべきものを取り違える誤解が生ずるが、誤解が生ずることすらも可能性に含んでいる点も、この仕組みの要点である。日本の国旗などはその好例かもしれない。

白地に赤い丸の受容力

日本の国旗は白地に赤い丸である。これはシンボルあるいはエンプティネスとは

何かを考える上で、格好の事例と言える。

赤い丸に意味はない。赤い丸は単に赤い丸である。それ以上でも以下でもない。これにたとえば、天皇であるとか、国家であるとか、愛国心などという意味を付与したとしても、それは恣意的なことである。比喩的に言えば、赤い丸は、目を引く存在であるから、この視覚的なオブジェクトに特定の意味を付与し、流通させれば、効率の良い視覚伝達が行われるだろう。赤い丸はさしあたって空っぽの器であるから、どんな意味でもそこに受け入れることができる。侵略と破壊も、帝国主義も、あるいは愛国心や平和という見立ても受け入れることができる。僕は戦後の日本に生まれたためにこれを平和国家のシンボルマークと教えられた。そういう話を中国の大学あたりですると、ざわざわと教室にざわめきが起きるので、これをそういう風に解釈することに違和感を覚える人々もいることが分かる。第二次世界大戦中に、この赤い丸を額の中央に巻き付けて多くの兵士が殺戮に与し、また戦死した事実を考慮すると、赤い丸という器の中には抜き差しならない中身が入り込んでしまったかもしれない。しかしながら、記号と意味の関係は常に恣意的である。これを国家と考えようと、神道を象徴する太陽であると考えようと、真心であると解釈しようと、白いご飯の上の梅干しであると考えようと、基本的には自由である。平和と教わった人々にはこれは平和に見える。しかしながら、赤い丸には、何度も言うようだが

白 ｜ 空白　エンプティネス

意味などない。それを誰がどう見立てるかという解釈のみがある。

白地に赤い丸の旗がはためく時、シンボルはそれを見る全ての人々の思いを残らず受けとめて機能する。オリンピックなどの表彰式でこれは、世界中の様々な人々の思いをあまねく受け入れて、掲揚され、大きな求心力を生む。この強烈な求心力がシンボルのコミュニケーション力である。つまりシンボルの本質は受容力、すなわちエンプティネスそのものである。

したがってシンボルの規模は、その受容力に比例する。白地に赤い丸は単純な造形で抽象度が高く、多義的であるために、実に多様なイメージを受け入れるシンボルとなる。白を背景とした赤い丸という構図は、地に対して図が何かを象徴する構図のひとつの典型である。丸は赤さそのものでなく、白とのコントラストにおいて赤い。赤が円であるということも、四角い背景とのコントラストを際立たせている。

赤、黒、白、青という日本の四原色については既に話したが、明、暗、顕、漠の中から、顕しい輝きの白に、燃え立つ赤を配した極大のコントラストがそこに出現している。

このような大きな受容力を持ったシンボルはそう多くはない。キリスト教の十字架はその仲間であるかもしれない。クロスは意識の明晰なフォーカスを促すシンボルである。

人の注目を集め、どんな意味をも受け入れる多大な受容力を持つ形質がシンボル

なのである。シンボルに善し悪しなどない。性能という観点に立てば、シンボルの出来不出来によって受容力の大小はあるかもしれない。しかしシンボルそのものは空っぽなので善いも悪いもない。もしあるとすればシンボルの潜在力をどう機能させるかという運用における可能性においてである。そして、たとえそこに負のイメージを受容せざるを得ない悲しい来歴があったとしても、再び希望を盛り込もうとする意志がそこに働くなら、受容力の大きなシンボルはそれら全てを受け入れるのである。悲しみも、屈辱も、希望も、平和も、相矛盾する多くの概念を黙して受容することで、日本の国旗は機能している。

空と白

空白の運用を意識的に行いはじめたその端緒を日本の歴史の中に探すと、室町中期の東山文化に眼が止まる。室町中期から桃山にかけて成立した茶の湯の美意識の発端に、空白の美が座っているのだ。本書のテーマは「白」であり「空」ではない。したがって、エンプティネスという力の運用にどこまで踏み込むかは微妙なところであるが、白と空とは非常に近接な関係を持っている。空白とはまさにこの二つを同時に語る概念である。白には「空」が、空には「白」が包含されている。だから

茶の湯における空の運用についてしばらく語るが、その中に白の概念を滑り込ませつつ読んでいただければ幸いである。

茶の湯

茶の道具は簡潔で美しい。手元にある茶入れは漆の溜塗りで、器の頭頂部は水が表面張力いっぱいに膨らんだような絶妙な曲面として周囲の光を集め、優美な光を放っている。茶杓も見るほどに吸い込まれるような繊細な形をしている。野にある竹をさっと小刀で削ったような、簡素なつくりであるが、竹の節をひとつアクセントとして配したその造形は、工夫をつくした素材と形の結果として自然と意識が緊張し、吸い寄せられるようである。

なぜ、簡潔さが美しく、強いのか、なぜ簡素さに感動が宿るのか。プレーンな造形に美を見出す日本の感性のメカニズムはどのような仕組みで成り立っているのか。そのようなことを少し考えてみたい。

古来、人間は、装飾の稠密性に意味や力、そして美を見出した。青銅器の昔、縄文土器の昔に始まり絶対王朝まで、中国もヨーロッパも、イスラムも密教も、人類史の大半は、複雑な紋様をものの上に張り巡らせ繁茂させることに力を注いできた。

稠密な紋様は強力な「力」の表象であり、人は村であれ国であれ、その集団のまとまりを維持していくための「力」の所在をはっきりと示す必要があった。したがって、優れた技芸をもってして、多大な時間をかけることでしか達成し得ない稠密な装飾紋様は、集団を統率する権力の表象として重用された。

だから、集団的動物である人類の歴史の上に現れた道具類は、はじめから複雑な装飾紋様で覆われていたのである。したがって、プレーンで簡素な青銅器などなく、青銅器の表面は、誕生の当初から緻密な紋様でびっしりと埋めつくされていた。龍紋をはじめとする中国の装飾やイスラムの幾何学パターン、バロックやロココなど絶対君主のための調度が緻密な造形で埋めつくされている理由も全て同じである。中国は龍紋をたぎらせ、イスラムは幾何学パターンを精緻に巡らせて、互いの文化の力と威を示しあっていたのである。

シンプルなものの様相に合理性を見つけ、そこに美や価値を意識したのは、西洋においてわずか百五十年ほど前のことである。頭上を覆っていた絶対権力が瓦解し、市民社会が訪れた。それは人がひとりひとり自分の主体性で生き方を選択し、生きる場所を選び、職業を選択できる社会であり、もはや大きな力の表象を必要としない社会であった。この近代社会の実現とともに、シンプル、最小、ミニマルといった合理性が称揚されるようになった。人が生きて環境をなす、その環境の形成にお

いて、資源の最大効率を意識した合理的な生産の美意識や問題解決の最短距離に意義を見出す価値観が浮上してくるのである。これはこれで腑に落ちる。

しかし日本は西洋のモダニズムに先駆けること数百年、室町時代の中期に、既に簡素さに美を見出す価値観を生み出していた。それはなぜか。

室町時代の中期、将軍足利義政は、それまでの日本文化の蓄積を焼き尽くす応仁の乱に倦んでいた。美に聡く文化に通じた義政にとっては、文化財の喪失は痛恨の出来事だったと推察される。

長い年月を経て醸成される信仰心や美意識、そして熟練の職人技術が何年何百年にもわたって注ぎ込まれることで実現する神社や仏閣。絢爛たる彩色や金銀が施された料紙に、修練を積んだ能書家が奇跡のような筆致で描いた詩や書画の数々。遠く霞む太古から営々と受け継がれ京の都に蓄積されてきたこれらの文物が、わずかひと世代の欲に起因する愚かな戦乱で、たやすく灰燼に帰する状況を目のあたりにして義政は何を思ったか。実際、応仁の乱は、僕らが史実からイメージするよりも遥かに壊滅的に日本文化の物的な蓄積を焼失させたようである。結果として義政は将軍職を息子に譲り、東山の地に隠居する。

義政が東山に築いた山荘が、通称銀閣として親しまれている慈照寺である。義政はここで静かに、書画や茶の湯などの趣味を深めていく時間を過ごした。ここに始

まる文化が「東山文化」と呼ばれるもので、ここから日本は新たな文化の局面を開いていくことになる。要するに、日本文化は応仁の乱を境に、一度リセットされ、義政の東山文化とともに再スタートを切る恰好になった。

このあたりに発生する美意識がなぜ「簡素」と「空白」をたずさえたか。義政をはじめ、戦乱に倦んだ当時の都人の胸に去来した心象が、ものの感じ方に影響を及ぼしたのかもしれない。しかし、そういう憶測にさしたる意味はない。いずれにしても、海を介して多様な渡来文化の影響を受け続けてきた日本が、その影響から微妙に身をよじるようにのがれはじめ、この時期から、簡素さの中に独自の美の感覚を模索しはじめたのである。

和室の原形

義政が多く時を過ごしたとされる慈照寺の一角、東求堂の同仁斎という書院は、極めて簡素でありながら、程よい緊張感に満たされた美しい空間である。畳は既に床に置くものではなく、部屋全体に敷きつめられて用いられている。同仁斎は四畳半という正方形の間である。

部屋の奥には書き物をする張台、その奥には明かり取りの障子がしつらえられて

白　空白　エンプティネス

いる。そこを開けると、庭の景観がぴしりと切り取られて眼前に現れる。張台の左には違い棚が設けられており、書物や、飾っておく道具の類いが配されていたと推測される。張台の右手で、その向こうは縁側になる。長いひさしが陰を作り、縁側に深い陰翳を宿す同仁斎に、障子越しの白い光が差し込む風情は、まぎれもなく日本の空間のひとつの原形である。部屋の他の二方は襖で構成されており、いわゆる「和室」と今日呼ばれている条件の全てがここにある。

茶室の源流とも呼ばれるこの簡潔な空間で、義政は茶を味わい、ひとり静かに心を遊ばせていた。

義政と茶で交わったとされる侘び茶の開祖、珠光もおそらくはこの部屋を訪れたはずである。珠光は豪華さや「唐物」を尊ぶ舶来志向を捨てて、冷え枯れたものの風情、すなわち「侘び」に美を見出した才能である。この珠光と義政は、同仁斎でどのような時間を過ごし、どんなイマジネーションを交換し合っていたのだろうか。

珠光を受け継ぎ茶の湯を進化させた武野紹鷗(たけのじょうおう)は「日本風」すなわち簡素な造形に複雑な人間の内面を託すものの見方を探求した。簡素さは空白に通じ、そこには様々な人の思いを入れておく余地が育まれる。これは日本の神話世界や空っぽにさせるコミュニケーションの仕組みと原理は同じである。茶杓は、竹の節がアクセントになるだけの単純なものである。これは紹鷗が考案した趣向と見られ、それまで

はどちらかと言えば象牙に複雑な装飾が施された唐物の茶杓などが珍重されてきた経緯を見ると、ここで明確に日本風が意識されはじめたことが分かる。

やがて千利休によって、茶の湯の空間や道具、作法はひとつの極まりへと導かれていく。簡素と沈黙。エンプティだからこそ、そこに何かを見ようとするイメージを招き入れることができる。人間の創造力による無辺の「見立て」を受容し、コミュニケーションの力へと変容させていく。それが茶の湯のコンセプトであり思想である。

利休の時代になると、茶室は極端に狭くなり、ほとんど無造作に作られたようなさりげなさが、見かけの簡素さとは逆に猛烈なエネルギーで意識化されるようになる。茶入れの器も、茶碗も、花の生け方も、極めて簡潔・明晰に澄んでくる。茶の湯を供する一連の所作も、手順を無駄にせず、しかも相手に誠意をつくす合理性のもとに整理され洗練の度を深めていく。

茶の湯は茶室という最小の空間で亭主が客をもてなし、互いの意を交流させる営みであるが、茶室が簡素であるのには理由がある。そこが空白であることによって、最小限のしつらいで、大きなイメージをそこに呼び入れることができるのだ。亭主は、床の間に生けた花と掛け軸に描かれた書画で一期一会の趣向を表現する。たとえば、水盤に水を張って、その水面に桜の花びらを浮かせて配するだけで、主客はあたか

も満開の桜の木の下に座っているかのような幻想を共有することができる。このような、しつらえられた表現を解釈し、そこに込められたメッセージを読み解いたり膨らませたりする行為を「見立て」という。一見みすぼらしい素の空間である茶室は、具象的な演出がないだけに、自在にどんなイマジネーションをも受け入れることができる。同じ茶室が、満開の桜の木の下になったり、波の打ち寄せる寂しい海辺になったり、深い井戸の底のように感じられたりするのである。

庭に咲き誇る朝顔を期待する秀吉をもてなすのに、逆に庭の朝顔を全て摘み取り、茶室の床に一輪だけ残して生けたという利休の逸話はあまりにも有名であるが、茶室は虚と実が人間の認識を介して変転していく形而上的な劇場として機能しているのである。

利休の茶室の対極にあるものはオペラやミュージカルの舞台かもしれない。舞台装置が現実の空間を写実的にあるいは誇張してそこにあることや、照明や音楽といった具体的な演出が人間の感覚を直接刺激して豊富なイマジネーションを湧出させる。それに対して茶の湯はできる限り何もしないことで、幻想をそこに呼び込むのである。

茶室に至る庭や、そのアプローチは、日常から非日常への移動空間である。手入れが行き届き緻密に制御された自然空間を経由することで、人間の感覚は次第に緊

張し、鋭敏に澄んでくる。結果としてもはやどんなに小さな変化も見逃さないほどに研ぎすまされた五感をたずさえた客が、茶室の中に座ることになる。したがってごくわずかの情報が、茶室内では雄弁なイメージの資源となる。

以下は茶の湯に関する利休の七か条の教えである。

花は野の花のように
炭は湯の沸くように
夏は涼しく
冬は暖かく
刻限ははやめに
降らずとも雨用意
相客に心をつけよ

たったこれだけかと思われるかもしれないが、これらの言葉から想起されるメタフォリカルな注意点はそれこそ無限にある。たとえば「花は野の花のように」は、野に咲いているようにさりげなく花を生けよという、花の生け方に関する留意を促しているが、花を生けるという営みが人為である以上、野にあるように花を生ける

白 ｜ 空白　エンプティネス

ことは不可能であり、成就できたという達成感は永久に得られないかもしれない。さらにこれを、花に限らず、命あるものや旬を考慮すべきもの全てに押し広げて解釈するならば、「野の花のように」それらを差配することは、さらに広範な意識の警句として低く大きく響く。

茶の湯は客に「茶を飲む」営みを供するもてなしであるが、これは人の営み総体の隠喩でもある。したがって、七か条の言葉は、人の営み全体に関与するさらに多様な見立てを促す余白をたずさえている。つまり見立て次第で、人ともの、人と人のあらゆる状況に意を通わせる発想の資源になる。そういう空白の原理がここにも機能しているのである。

発想は空白に宿る

空白を資源とすることで、様々なコミュニケーションや創造的な意思の疎通ができることについて述べてきた。空白がそこに存在することで、それを補完しようと頭脳が運動する。そこにコミュニケーションや思考が発生するのである。さらに言えば、「考える」あるいは、発想するという脳の営みそのものも、「問い」に無意識に反応すること、「思う」という能動性によってゼロから構築的に作られるのではなく、

とで成立するのではないかと僕は考えている。「我思う」の前に、目に見えない「問い」を置く。問いとは脳の中に何らかの拍子に生まれる空白である。

不完全を承知でひとつのたとえ話をしよう。「椀子そば」というものをご存じだろうか。「椀子そば」とは、椀に入れられたそばを素早く食べると、傍らにいるお給仕さんが空いた椀に、すかさずひと椀分のそばを投入する。それをまた素早く食べると、間髪を入れず次のひと椀分が空いた椀に投入される。そばはほとんどひと口で啜れる分量なので、次々にこれが継続されていく。景気のいい合いの手をお給仕さんたちが入れるので、食べる方は、そのリズムに煽(あお)られて、食べる速度を自分でコントロールするのが難しい。お給仕さんたちは、空になった器を、次々と客の目の前に積んでいく。それが少しずつ高くなる。客は、それを横目で見ながら、そこはかとなくある種の達成感や記録への挑戦を意識しつつ、自分の満腹の限界まで食べるのである。うずたかく積まれた椀の集積は何かを成し遂げた成果物に見える。

考える、という行為は逆回しの「椀子そば」のようなものだ。つまり、目の前に次々に差し出される空っぽの椀に、脳が、「そば」ならぬ「思考」を次々と入れていくような感じである。タイミングよく差し出された空の椀に、間髪を入れず「思考」をひとつ置く、次の空の椀にまたひとつ……。これを条件反射のように繰り返していくうちに「思考」はやがてうずたかく、目の前に堆積していくのである。なぜ、ど

白 ｜ 空白　エンプティネス

のような経緯でこのような思考の堆積物が生産されたのかは分からないが、連続的に差し出された小さな空の器に、この成果を媒介している。つまり、脳は、差し出された小さな空の器に、反射的に「答」を入れるという傾向を持っている。思考や発想は、「空白の器」が媒介しているのである。

独創的な問いに答は不要

沈黙こそ雄弁である。ここまで語ってくることで、このような一見矛盾に満ちた言葉も、単なる反語ではなく充分な説得力を持って響いてくるはずだ。ただの饒舌はむしろ言葉の価値を下落させ、意味のインフレーションを引き起こす。有効に用いられる沈黙こそ意味の価値を担保し、そこに叡智を呼び起こす思考やコミュニケーションの要なのである。

一方で、「Simple is Best.」とか「Less is More.」などと言われる発想の根は、空白やエンプティネスとは微妙に異なるものである。エンプティネスは単に造形的な簡素さや合理的に洗練されているというだけのものではない。そこには自由な想像力を許容するスペースがあり、それを活用することで、認識の形成や意思の疎通が何倍も豊かになる。その可能性が、エンプティネスである。だから、単に幾何学的に

単調なスタイリングに固執したり、意識的に無口を装ってみてもうまくは行かない。空白やエンプティネスの運用には、やはり修練と経験が不可欠である。シンプル・単純ではなく、機能する空白を使わなくてはいけない。自在なイマジネーションを招き入れる潜在力そのものが意のままにプランニングできれば完璧だ。独創性とはエンプティネスの覚醒力、すなわち問いの質のことである。独創的な問いこそが「表現」と呼ぶにふさわしく、そこに限定された答は必要ない。それは既に無数の答を蔵しているのであるから。

第四章

白へ

推敲

白は、完成度というものに対する人間の意識に影響を与え続けた。紙と印刷の文化に関係する美意識は、文字や活字の問題だけではなく、言葉をいかなる完成度で定着させるかという、情報の仕上げと始末への意識を生み出している。白い紙に黒いインクで文字を印刷するという行為は、不可逆な定着をおのずと成立させてしまうので、未成熟なもの、吟味の足らないものはその上に発露されてはならないという、暗黙の了解をいざなう。

推敲という言葉がある。推敲とは中国の唐代の詩人、賈島（かとう）の、詩作における逡巡の逸話である。詩人は求める詩想において「僧は推（お）す月下の門」がいいか「僧は敲（たた）く月下の門」がいいかを決めかねて悩む。逸話が逸話たるゆえんは、選択する言葉のわずかな差異と、その微差において詩のイマジネーションになるほど大きな変容が起こり得るという共感が、この有名な逡巡を通して成立するということであろう。月あかりの静謐な風景の中を、音もなく門を推すのか、あるいは静寂の中に木戸を

敲く音を響かせるかは、確かに大きな違いかもしれない。いずれかを決めかねる詩人のデリケートな感受性に、人はささやかな同意を寄せるかもしれない。しかしながら一方で、推すにしても敲くにしても、それほどの逡巡を生み出すほどの大事でもなかろうという、微差に執着する詩人の神経質さ、器量の小ささをも同時に印象づけているかもしれない。これは「定着」あるいは「完成」という状態を前にした人間の心理に言及する問題である。

白い紙に記されたものは不可逆である。後戻りが出来ない。今日、押印したりサインしたりという行為が、意思決定の証として社会の中を流通している背景には、白い紙の上には訂正不能な出来事が固定されるというイマジネーションがある。白い紙の上に朱の印泥を用いて印を押すという行為は、明らかに不可逆性の象徴である。

思索を言葉として定着させる行為もまた白い紙の上にペンや筆で書くという不可逆性、そして活字として書籍の上に定着させるというさらに大きな不可逆性を発生させる営みである。推敲という行為はそうした不可逆性が生み出した営みであり美意識であろう。このような、達成を意識した完成度や洗練を求める気持ちの背景に、白という感受性が潜んでいる。

子供の頃、習字の練習は半紙という紙の上で行った。黒い墨で白い半紙の上に未

成熟な文字を果てしなく発露し続ける、その反復が文字を書くトレーニングであった。取り返しのつかないつたない結末を紙の上に顕し続ける呵責の念が上達のエネルギーとなる。練習用の半紙といえども、白い紙である。そこに自分のつたない行為の痕跡を残し続けていく。紙がもったいないというよりも、白い紙に消し去れない過失を累積していく様を把握し続けることが、おのずと推敲という美意識を加速させるのである。この、推敲という意識をいざなう推進力のようなものが、紙を中心としたひとつの文化を作り上げてきたのではないかと思うのである。もしも、無限の過失をなんの代償もなく受け入れ続けてくれるメディアがあったとしたならば、推すか敲くかを逡巡する心理は生まれてこないかもしれない。

現代はインターネットという新たな思考経路が生まれた。ネットというメディアは一見、個人のつぶやきの集積のようにも見える。しかし、ネットの本質はむしろ、不完全を前提にした個の集積の向こう側に、皆が共有できる総合知のようなものに手を伸ばすことのように思われる。つまりネットを介してひとりひとりが考えるという発想を超えて、世界の人々が同時に考えるというような状況が生まれつつある。かつては、百科事典のような厳密さの問われる情報の体系を編むにも、個々のパートは専門家としての個の書き手がこれを担ってきた。しかし現在では、あらゆる人々が加筆訂正できる百科事典のようなものがネットの中を動いている。間違いやいた

ずら、思い違いや表現の不的確さは、世界中の人々の眼に常にさらされている。印刷物を間違いなく世に送り出す時の意識とは異なるプレッシャー、良識も悪意も、嘲笑も尊敬も、揶揄も批評も一緒にした興味と関心が生み出す知の圧力によって、情報はある意味で無限に更新を繰り返しているのだ。無数の人々の眼にさらされ続ける情報は、変化する現実に限りなく接近し、寄り添い続けるだろう。断定しない言説に真偽がつけられないように、その情報はあらゆる評価を回避しながら、文体を持たないニュートラルな言葉で知の平均値を示し続けるのである。明らかに、推敲がもたらす質とは異なる、新たな知の基準がここに生まれようとしている。

白への跳躍

しかしながら、無限の更新を続ける情報には「清書」や「仕上がる」というような価値観や美意識が存在しない。無限に更新され続ける巨大な情報のうねりが、知の圧力として情報にプレッシャーを与え続けている状況では、情報は常に途上であり終わりがない。

一方、紙の上に乗るということは、黒いインクなり墨なりを付着させるという、後戻りできない状況へ乗り出し、完結した情報を成就させる仕上げへの跳躍を意味

する。白い紙の上に決然と明確な表現を屹立させること。不可逆性を伴うがゆえに、達成には感動が生まれる。またそこには切り口の鮮やかさが発現する。その営みは、書や絵画、詩歌、音楽演奏、舞踊、武道のようなものに顕著に現れている。手の誤り、身体のぶれ、鍛錬の未熟さを超克し、失敗への危険に臆することなく潔く発せられる表現の強さが、感動の根源となり、諸芸術の感覚を鍛える暗黙の基礎となってきた。音楽や舞踊における「本番」という時間は、真っ白な紙と同様の意味をなす。聴衆や観衆を前にした時空は、まさに「タブラ・ラサ」、白く澄みわたった紙である。弓矢の初級者に向けた忠告として「諸矢を手挟みて的に向かふ」ことをいさめる逸話が『徒然草』にある。標的に向かう時に二本目の矢を持って弓を構えてはいけない。その刹那に訪れる二の矢への無意識の依存が一の矢への切実な集中を鈍らせるという指摘である。この、矢を一本だけ持って的に向かう集中の中に白がある。

清掃

美しさは創造の領域に属するものと考えられがちだが、何かを生み出すのではなく、ものを掃き清め、拭き清めて、清楚を維持するという営みそのものの中に、むしろ見出されるものではないかと最近では思うようになった。特に、禅宗の寺や庭

などに触れるにつけ、その思いは強くなる。禅寺の庭が美しいのは、作庭家の才につきるものではない。むしろ常に掃き清められ、手をかけられているがゆえの美しさとも見える。それも一年や二年の清掃ではなく、長い年月を経て、清掃に清掃を重ねてくることで、自然と人間の営みの、どちらともつかない領域におのずと生まれてくる造形の波打ち際のようなものが、庭というものの本質をなしているように感じられるのだ。

自然とは変化流転するものであり、人為を超えて強靭で、それは人間の思惑のうちにとどまらない。岩や地面には苔が生じ、落ち葉は堆積して新たな土を作る。木肌は退色して滋味を生じ、池の水は碧に澄む。自然の贈与を受け入れることは、待つということである。長い時間の果てに、人為ではとうてい届かない自然の恵みに浴すことが出来る。

一方で、人は意志を持って、自然と拮抗するものである。禅寺の方丈の前に広がる白い四角い石庭は、人の意志の象徴にも見える。有機的な自然の中に決然と白く四角く存在を示している。この白い石の庭は自然のままでは維持することができない。放っておくと、落ち葉や大然の塵芥がその上にゆっくりと降り注ぎ、アースカラーに覆われていく。その白を白として保つには、小さな石のおびただしい集積の中に混入した自然の微細な塵芥を取り払い、ぬぐい去るという、気の遠くなるほど手間

のかかる作業が必要になる。もちろん、石庭に限らず、飛び石も、苔も、床も、障壁も、埃を拭い、ちりを払い、自然の風化に任せない人為による制御を、倦まず撓まず繰り返さないと庭は維持できない。自然のままに放置すると、禅寺は数年のうちに草木に埋もれて朽ち果てるだろう。そのような、自然と人為のせめぎあい、あるいは混沌と秩序のせめぎあいが清掃である。その清掃の果てに現れてくる人と自然のあわいに日本の庭がある。

また、清掃は創造を伴わないという点では、変化ではなく維持に価値をおく態度でもある。今日においては諸芸術全般に「新しさ」すなわち刷新性をことさら評価する風潮があるが、誤解を恐れずに言えば、日本の美意識とは新しさを生み出すことよりもむしろ維持するところに湧き出した心性ではないかと思うのである。変化の激しいのは今日のみではない。自然は常に流動する。その流動を食い止め、静止を意図し、普遍と不変を標榜しながらコンシステンシーを保っていくことには壮大なエネルギーが必要である。禅寺という場所はそういう意味での常態不変への意志で制御し、日々清掃を重ねている。その常態不変の象徴のように見える石庭が、白く表現されていることは重要である。

未知化

　ある対象について深く考えることによって、その対象が、まるで初めて見るかのような新鮮さを取り戻すことがある。書き慣れた文字も、反復して書くうちに、不思議な造形物のように感じられてくることがある。その刹那、僕らは異国人がはじめて日本の文字に触れた時の新鮮さと同じものを感じ取っているはずだ。
　僕らは「花」について多くの経験をしすぎているがゆえに、花のリアリティが分からなくなっている。しかしたとえば、一枚の写真が、花は明らかに生殖器である事実を目の前に示すことで、僕らは自分たちの目についたウロコを落とすことができる。多くの才能ある写真家が競って花の写真を撮るのは、花が美しいからではない。人の心を動かしてやまないその対象物を、未だかつて誰もが捉え得なかったイメージとして捉え直すことに惹かれてやまないからである。生まれて初めて花を見るような鮮烈な感動を、静止した画像として成就させる情熱に憑かれてやまないからである。石元泰博の花の写真に、あるいはロバート・メイプルソープの花の写真を通して、僕らは花のイメージを未知なるものへと更新することができる。
　未知化とはそういう現象である。既知化し惰性化した知識を、根源の方に戻して感じ直してみることで、僕らは新鮮にものごとを認識し直すことができる。「分かる」

とは元来、そういうことだったのではないだろうか。さらに言えば、そのような「未知化」を意図的に行い、「分かる」を成就させることの中に表現の本質があるのではないかと思うのである。

未知化は白に通じている。白とは混沌に向かう力に逆行し、突出してくるイメージの特異点である。それは既知の混濁から身をよじり、鮮度のある情報の形としてくっきりと僕らの意識の中に立ち上がる。白とは、汚れのない認識である。いとしろしき様相の具現、情報の屹立した様を言う。いとしろしき様相はいとしろしき認識を呼び起こす。「分かる」とは「いとしろしき認識」そのものではないか。既知化し、惰性化することは、意識の屹立がおさえられ認識の泥沼に沈むことである。その泥沼から、まっさらの白い紙のような意識を取り出してくることが「分かる」ということである。

僕らは世界に対しては永久に無知である。そしてそれでいいのだ。世界のリアリティに無限におののき続けられる感受性を創造性と呼ぶのだから。

白砂と月光

慈照寺は、枯淡の風情に人気があり、常に多くの参拝者を引きつけてやまない。

寺社の建築や作庭の妙、書院の趣、向月台や銀沙灘の造形など、この寺の魅力は枚挙にいとまがない。しかし、この寺が、人々の心に刻印するものは、時を超え、時代を超えて残ってきた日本の美の核心のようなものだ。清掃に清掃を重ねる一方で、自然はこの寺のきらびやかなものを一枚一枚はぎ取るように風化させてきた。結果として現れてきた枯淡の風情を、人は慈しみ、さらに清掃を重ねてその美を絶やさぬように維持してきた。

この寺の美しさは、月の美しさに似ている。月は日の光を受けてしんと澄んで世界を照らす。二階建ての銀閣はこの寺の中心的な建物だが、その下層を「心空殿」といい、二層を「潮音閣」という。潮音閣には観音像が祀られている。この寺の清掃や手入れを営む職人は、定年を迎える日に一度だけ、潮音閣に登ることを許される。潮音閣から庭を見おろす。長い年月をかけて清掃を重ね、自然を呼び込み、また自然の浸食から守ってきた庭である。銀沙灘と呼ばれる海のような白砂の広がりの上に、波のような文様が描かれている様子が月の光に照らされる。それは息をのむように白いという。

白 ｜ 白へ

あとがき

目を覚まして庭を見ると雪であった。雪は寝床にいるときから気配で分かる。何かがしんしんと世界に積もっていく密やかな堆積感を、体のどこかが感じている。窓を開けると別世界が燦然（さんぜん）と現れる。なんという光景をこの世は持っているのだろう。水蒸気が空気中のちりを核にして雪の結晶となる。そしてそれは目覚ましく白い。

そういうものがおびただしく降り注いで世界を覆い尽くしている。

近年、建築や都市、人や言葉は、どこか半透明になってきた。建築はガラスや新素材で存在感が軽くなり、インターネット上を飛び交う言葉は、立ちも座りもせず浮遊している。それは知らぬ間に更新されているか、あるいは古色もつかないまっさらの様相で何年も存在し続ける。そんな状況に新鮮さや可能性を感じて、それをさらに拡張しようと僕らは日々努力を続けている。おそらくこの半透明の世界は今後も増殖を続けるだろう。やがて僕らの意識の大半は、そこに住まうことになるのかもしれない。

しかし、こうして雪に遭遇する。それは手の平に静かに舞い降り、溶けて光の露となる。僕らは、消すことも、更新することも、半透明にすることもできないこの

身体を通して、白の摂理に感じ入るのだ。

雪は当分やむ気配がない。

二〇〇八年二月三日

追記

本書は、当初より中央公論新社の松本佳代子さんに興味を注ぎ続けていただいたことが推進力となった。ライターの橋本麻里さんから折に触れて白にまつわるいくつかのエピソードを聞かせていただいたことも筆の助けとなった。茶の湯の師匠、千宗屋さんから教わった樂焼、特に長次郎の黒樂の世界は、白を考えるうえで貴重なイメージの対照となった。掲載した樂茶碗の写真は、陰翳から浮かび上がる黎明の白のイメージだが、これは写真家の上田義彦さんに撮り下ろしてもらった。慈照寺（銀閣）同仁斎脇の石庭の写真も上田さんの撮り下ろしである。樂美術館には黒樂「勾当」の撮影をさせていただいた。さらに、白い花の写真は写真家の石元泰博さんの作品集『花』の中の一作「泰山木」を掲載させていただいた。石元さんが掲載に快く応じてくださり、プリントしてくださったご厚意には感激し、敬服した。ご協力いただいた方々にはここで改めてお礼を申しあげたい。

また、世界を更新していくイマジネーションを、僕は武蔵野美術大学名誉教授の向井周太郎さんから常にいただいている。本書に述べた「紙の白さと張り」に関しては、その高著『ふすま』に触発されるものがあった。英訳については、翻訳をお願いしたヨーク大学のイ・ジュヨンさん、そして監訳・編集をして下さった同大学のテッド・グーセンさんの文学的な翻訳のクオリティに感謝したい。これで本書は英語圏の人々にも触れていただけるようになった。

本書の第一章は拙著『デザインのデザイン／Special Edition』にも同様の内容が収録されている。本書を書きつつも、「白」を巡る着想を、多くの図版や作品とともに紹介してみたかったからである。つまり「白」は自分のデザイン活動のコンセプトの一環として機能しはじめている。ある意味では、自分のデザインのよりどころのひとつが「白」なのかもしれない。

原研哉(はら・けんや)

一九五八年生まれ。グラフィックデザイナー。武蔵野美術大学教授。「もの」と同様に「こと」のデザインを志向している。世界各地を巡回し、広く影響を与えた「RE-DESIGN: 日常の二十一世紀」展(世界インダストリアルデザインビエンナーレ、インダストリアルデザインビエンナーレ、毎日デザイン賞受賞)をはじめとして「HAPTIC」「SENSEWARE」など既存の価値観を更新するキーワードを擁する展覧会を制作。また、長野オリンピックの開・閉会式プログラムや、愛知万博のプロモーションでは、深く日本文化に根ざしたデザインを展開した。二〇〇二年より、無印良品のアートディレクションを担当。酒や珈琲の商品デザインのほか、松屋銀座、森ビル、蔦屋書店、GINZA SIX などの VI を手がける。一連の活動によって内外のデザイン賞を多数受賞。著書『デザインのデザイン』(岩波書店、二〇〇三年)は、サントリー学芸賞を受賞。同書は中国・韓国・台湾語に翻訳された後、大幅な増補を加えた英語版『DESIGNING DESIGN』(Lars Müller Publishers, 2007) として出版され、世界に多くの読者を持つ。ほかに『日本のデザイン』(岩波新書、二〇一一年)、『百百』(中央公論新社、二〇一八年)、『低空飛行』(岩波書店、二〇二二年) など著書多数。二〇二四年紫綬褒章受章。

白(しろ)

原研哉

二〇〇八年五月三十日初版発行
二〇二五年二月二十日十版発行

発行者　安部順一

発行所　中央公論新社
〒一〇〇-八一五二　東京都千代田区大手町一-七-一
電話
販売〇三-五二九九-一七三〇
編集〇三-五二九九-一七四〇
https://www.chuko.co.jp/

印刷
本文：三晃印刷
写真：サンエムカラー
カバー：大熊整美堂

製本　小泉製本

©2008 Kenya HARA
Published by CHUOKORON-SHINSHA, INC.
Printed in Japan

ISBN 978-4-12-003937-9 C0070

定価はカバーに表示してあります。
落丁本・乱丁本はお手数ですが小社販売部宛にお送りください。送料小社負担にてお取り替えいたします。

Kenya Hara
Born in 1958. Graphic designer; Professor at the Musashino Art university. Art director of MUJI since 2002. Kenya Hara is interested in designing "circumstances" or "conditions" rather than "things."

He traveled the world widely in an attempt to investigate the meaning of "design." These efforts were crystallized in the international touring exhibits, "RE-DESIGN," "HAPTIC," and "SENSEWARE"; each title representing a keyword that embraces the ever-changing value of existence. He incorporated traditional Japanese cultural features in designing the opening and closing ceremonies of the Nagano Winter Olympics, as well as in the promotion of the Aichi EXPO. He has designed commercial products for many companies including AGF, JT, KENZO, was involved in the renewal project of the Ginza branch of Matsuya department store, and worked on the sign design for Mori building VI and DAIKANYAMA TSUTAYA BOOKS.

He has received numerous design awards including the Japanese Cultural Design Award. His book, *Design of Design* (Iwanami Shoten, 2003) received the Suntory Arts and Science Award, and its new revised and expanded English edition, *DESIGNING DESIGN* (Lars Müller Publishers, Switzerland, 2007) found readers all over the world.

WHITE

First published on May 30, 2008
Reprinted on February 20, 2025

Author	Kenya Hara
Translator	Jooyeon Rhee
Translation Editor	Ted Goossen
Publishing	Junichi Abe
	Chuokoron-Shinsha, Inc.
	1-7-1 Otemachi, Chiyoda-ku, Tokyo
	100-8152, Japan
	https://www.chuko.co.jp/
Printing	Text: Sanko Printing
	Photo: Sun M Color
	Cover: Okumaseibido
Binding	Koizumi Book Binding
	©2008 Kenya HARA
	Published by CHUOKORON-SHINSHA, INC.
	Printed in Japan

ISBN 978-4-12-003937-9 C0070

Acknowledgements

This book has benefited from the constant support and encouragement of my editor, Matsumoto Kayoko of Chuokoron-Shinsha, Inc.. I was also aided by the writer Hashimoto Mari, who regaled me with anecdotes about white whenever the chance arose. The tea master, Sen So-oku, introduced me to the world of raku ware, especially the black raku produced by Chojiro I, whose art guided me to meditate on white. The picture of his piece, which evokes the image of white emerging from shadow, was photographed by Ueda Yoshihiko. Ueda-san is also responsible for the photograph of the stone garden from *Dojinsai* at the Silver Pavilion (*Ginkaku*). The image of the black raku ware entitled "Koto" was made available through the courtesy of the Raku Museum. Also, the image of the white flower, "Taisanboku" (Southern Magnolia) was taken from Ishimoto Yasuhiro's photo collection, *Hana* (Flower). I would like to express my deep gratitude to Ishimoto-san, who cheerfully gave me the print when asked. Finally, I would like to express my sincere thanks to all the other people who helped me complete this book.

Mukai Shutaro, Professor Emeritus at the Musashino Art University, has imparted his imaginative ideas about global renewal to me over the years. In particular, his book *Fusuma* (sliding doors) led me to develop the section, "whiteness and resilience of paper." I would also like to thank my translator, Jooyeon Rhee, and her editor, Ted Goossen, for striving to give the English version a literary flavor. It is my hope that, through their efforts, this book will be able to reach English-speaking readers.

The text of Chapter One overlaps somewhat with my previous book, *Designing Design*. This is because I wanted to introduce my approach to white using the many new illustrations made available in this edition. Finally, it seems that "white" has become a key link in my conceptual framework, and one of the foundational elements in my design.

Epilogue

When I opened my eyes this morning the garden was covered in snow. I had sensed that it was falling during the night. Some part of my body had been secretly registering that accumulation, the fact that something was quietly building up outside. I opened my window to a bright new world. How amazing are the many vistas this planet has to offer us! When precipitation in the air freezes, it turns to snow. The crystallized ice particles are stunningly white. They blanket the entire landscape.

    In recent years, so many things – architecture and cities, people and words – seem to have become semi-transparent. Perhaps I should rather say that they feel as if they are only half there. Architecture feels lighter because of its use of glass and other new building materials, while the words that traverse the Net float about in limbo, with no real place to call home. Will they be somehow renewed unbeknownst to us? Or will they maintain their fresh appearance for years, without ever acquiring the patina of age? We struggle on day after day, attempting to expand the freshness and the promise we feel in this new reality. After all, this semi-transparent world is likely to go on growing. Perhaps the greater part of our conscious minds will end up residing there.

    Yet the snow keeps falling. Flakes silently dance down to rest in my palm, where they melt into drops of light. White still has the power to bestow its divine grace upon these bodies of ours, which can neither disappear, nor renew themselves, nor turn semi-transparent.

    It looks like the snow will go on falling for a while.

February 3, 2008

Looking down from Cho-onkaku, one sees a garden preserved from natural erosion through a continuing process of cleaning and refining. The raked sand, the so-called "Sea of Silver Sand," shines in the moonlight; an image that truly reminds us of the ocean. The whiteness of the sand takes our breath away.

that the attempt to create "unfamiliar" objects is the essence of the creativity that leads us to "understand" things in this world.

Defamiliarization is closely related to white. White moves in the opposite direction of chaos; it is the singular image that emerges from disorder. White lies in our consciousness as fresh information escaped from our established world of knowledge. It cannot be corrupted or soiled; it forms the condition of *itoshiroshiki*, and it establishes information. The *itoshiroshiki* condition creates an awareness of *itoshiroshiki*. Doesn't "to understand" actually refer to our "consciousness of *itoshiroshiki*"? When "knowledge" and other habitual ways of thinking about things sink to the bottom of our consciousness, that thing we call "understanding" floats to the surface like pure white paper.

White Sand and Moonlight

The Silver Pavilion is famous worldwide for its simplicity and refinement, attracting a steady stream of visitors throughout the year. Its beauty is found in features like the splendid structure of the temple, the miracle of making garden, the elegant study room, *Kogetsudai*; the moon-viewing platform, *Ginsadan*; the garden with its sea of silver sand–the list goes on and on. Yet what leaves the strongest impression is the fact that this temple stands as the core of the Japanese aesthetic, which transcends time and historical era. Cleaned day after day, weathered over time, its natural beauty is revealed as it ages, as if it were stripping off its veils one after another. Moved by this simple yet refined work of art, people have tried to preserve its cultivated natural beauty through cleaning and polishing.

The beauty of the temple resembles the beauty of the moon. The moon quietly bathes the world in the reflected light of the sun. The two-storey Silver Pavilion forms the Temple's center; its first floor is called the "Shinkuden" (the Hall of Empty Heart), while the second floor is called the "Cho-onkaku" (the Hall of Roaring Waves). A statue of the bodhisattva Kannon is enshrined in the Cho-onkaku. It is said that temple staff who look after all the necessary maintenance are allowed to enter the Cho-onkaku only once before they retire.

to preservation than newness. I don't mean that Japanese are not creative; rather I think that innovation comes from that consciousness that tries to maintain things as they are. The power of transformation is not something new; nature transforms itself continuously. It requires much energy and consistency to preserve beautiful things, so we must observe transforming nature closely, capturing its stillness while advocating its immutable and universal features. In this sense, Zen temples are instructive, for they embody the commitment that is needed to preserve beauty through daily effort. Their pebbled white gardens can be taken as symbols of this principal of preservation.

Defamiliarization

When I meditate on an object, it becomes refreshingly different, as if I had just encountered it for the first time. Even during the repetitive process of writing, I can discover something unusual in characters I have used so many times before. In moments like this, we must feel some of the freshness that foreigners experience when they encounter Japanese characters for the first time.

Because we are so used to seeing "flowers" in everyday life, we fail to comprehend their essential nature. Yet if we perceive a flower as a living entity, even in a picture, we can come closer to reading its true essence. Photographers often compete to take pictures of flowers for reasons that have nothing to do with their beauty. Rather, they desire to reach the point where they can capture the living flowers in a way that no one ever has before. Obsessed by the idea of freezing such a unique image in their art, they wait passionately for that inspiring moment when flowers bloom. The photographs produced by Yasuhiro Ishimoto (1921-) and Robert Mapplethorpe (1946-1989), for example, show us how ordinary flowers can be transformed into something unfamiliar and unknown.

Such "defamiliarized" images mark the works of Mapplethorpe. Going back to the source of our acquired knowledge allows us to perceive things in a new light. I wonder whether the original meaning of "to understand" refers to this situation. To carry my point one step further, I think

tures that were created by a talented designer; rather, its beauty is uncovered through the continual process of cleaning. Refined beauty cannot be produced by short-term effort – it can only be established through a long process of cleaning and polishing that enables a human being and his natural surroundings to co-exist as one body. I can find this condition in a Zen temple garden, which is designed to convey the impression of a seashore.

Nature is always transforming itself, and its innate strength is far more powerful than we can imagine. Rocks, moss, and fallen leaves turn to soil over a long passage of time. The color of tree bark fades and then is reborn as new – the water in a pond is a clear blue. What we receive from nature is a blessing; we can immerse ourselves in something that cannot possibly be matched by human artifice.

On the one hand, human beings try to compete against the beauty of nature by consciously applying their creative willpower. This consciousness is symbolized in the spacious temple garden laid out before an abbot's chamber. The rectangular rock garden exists as a part of organic nature. The white pebbles in the garden, however, require constant care; if neglected, their whiteness soon takes on the color of earth, and the white ground of the garden is quickly covered by fallen leaves and dirt. In order to preserve this whiteness, the soil that naturally accumulates between the pebbles must be removed, a job that requires great time and energy. Of course, this cleaning work is not confined to the pebbles alone; the stepping-stones, moss, floors, and walls must be cleaned as well. In short, the garden is maintained by an unending human struggle against the weathering process of nature. If efforts are not made to preserve these features, the temple garden will become covered by grass in a year or two, and then begin to decay. In this struggle to preserve order from chaos, human beings and nature exist without boundaries. The Japanese garden embodies this delicate coexistence of mankind and nature.

On the other hand, though, insofar as creativity and maintenance are seen as unrelated entities, more recognition needs to be given to the cleaning process. Today's artists are accustomed to the current tide that assigns value to the creation of "something new." At the risk of being misunderstood, though, I think the Japanese sensibility is probably more attuned

A Leap toward White

Within the Net's realm of ever-changing information, value-laden principles such as "clean copy" and "completion" no longer apply. Information can no longer be concrete and clear because of the intellectual pressures that shape the Net, where knowledge, so to speak, is always unstable.

One condition of paper-based publishing is that ink cannot be erased once it's printed; a situation that allowed the principle of perfecting information to take a great leap forward. In other words, because of this condition we have established a system of decisive and precise expression on white paper. Its very irreversible nature means that we are emotionally moved when we achieve something on it. It constantly challenges us to come up with fresh forms, which feed into activities such as writing, painting, poetry, music, dance, and the martial arts. It is the possibility of (irrevocable) failure that lies behind all this creative energy. At the same time, the basis of the artistic mind is the overcoming of human error through strenuous practice and training. The moment before a performance of music or dance begins, for example, greatly resembles the purity of white paper; it is a state of tabula rasa for audience and performer, the perfectly white tablet.

The 14th century Japanese classic, *Tsurezuregusa* (translated as Essays in Idleness) by Yoshida Kenko (1283-1350) contains a famous attack on the teaching that you should, "carry two arrows in your hand when facing the target." An archer should carry only one arrow, Kenko admonishes; if he carries two, his concentration will be hampered by his unconscious dependence on the second one. It is within this total focus required of the archer that we encounter white.

Cleaning

It is easy to think that beauty resides in the realm of creative activity. Yet beauty hardly "appears" from nowhere. Recently, I have come to believe that we "discover" it through the cleaning and polishing we do to preserve things as they are. This feeling grows especially strong when I look at Zen temple gardens. The beauty of a temple garden rests not in the splendid fea-

countless times on the most common sort of Japanese paper. This kind of repetition was *shuji*; a kind of calligraphic training, even though my hand was clumsy and immature; in fact, the agony of writing such unattractive characters over and over on the pure white paper eventually inspired me to improve, although the paper preserved the record of my futility. In a similar way, perhaps, Kato's unrelenting attention to his own irreversible errors accelerated the aesthetic of *suiko*. I believe that the idea of *suiko* is one of the driving forces behind our paper-related culture. If we were using a medium that allowed us to slip our errors and mistakes through, we would never have been as focused on repetition and perfection – the push and the pull, as it were – as we are.

Today we live in a new thought processing system called the Internet. As an integrative media, the Net seems to have established a space to display the grumblings of the dissatisfied. Yet the true nature of Net is that it enables people to co-own synthetic knowledge despite the presupposition of the imperfections introduced by participating individuals. Each individual, whoever they are and wherever they may be in the world, is invited to express his or her thoughts. In the past, experts in each different field were responsible for organizing scrupulously detailed information systems like the encyclopedia. However, something similar to the process of editing an encyclopedia happens on the Net; anyone can touch up and correct information. Incorrect or useless information, heterodox opinions and inappropriate expressions – all are being exposed to people all over the world instantaneously. Information on the Net is continuously revised, acquiring an infinite number of meanings as people express their interests and curiosity in a wide variety of forums. We find a mix of good and bad knowledge, of malicious intent, and of scorn, respect, ridicule, criticism, and so on. The pressures we see on the Net are quite unlike those in the world of publishing. Perhaps that is because this constantly changing store of information is so close to our daily life. Such information doesn't bear the burden of criticism; rather, it standardizes knowledge through the use of a neutral language, as if it were trying to hide its true intention. Clearly, a new standard of knowledge is being born on the Net, in a world far removed from the aesthetic of *suiko*.

Suiko and the Irreversible Text

White influences people's relationship to the idea of completeness, and perfection. The aesthetic principles of cultures built up around paper and printing go far beyond print and typefaces; they produce a consciousness that seeks to control information through the so-called perfection of language. The irreversible act of printing black letters on white paper carries with it a tacit understanding that those texts that are immature, or that have not been adequately scrutinized, will not be so exposed.

There is a word, pronounced *suiko* in Japanese, which originates from a story well known throughout East Asia. The story involves a Chinese poet, Kato (*Bai-Dau*, 779-843), who lived during the Tang dynasty. One day, Kato was having an especially hard time deciding how to complete the last part of his poem. Should he use the phrase "a monk pushes (*sui*) the door in the moonlight," or "a monk knocks on (*ko*) the door in the moonlight"? Try as he might, he found it impossible to resolve the problem. Now this is just an anecdote, yet it demonstrates how subtle differences between words shape the poetic imagination. Perhaps we think there is no difference whether the monk pushes the door or knocks on it. Perhaps we are impressed by the delicate sensitivity that led to his indecision. Or we may question the narrow-mindedness that caused him to agonize over a seemingly trivial detail. Whichever the case, though, we are dealing with the psychological need to obtain "fixity" and "perfection."

One cannot erase things once they have been written on paper. There is no going back. Today, this kind of imagination can be found in the socially accepted act of acknowledging a document by affixing one's seal or signature to it. The act of stamping a red seal clearly symbolizes this irreversibility.

It is an irreversible move to fix one's thoughts by writing them down on white paper, and an even more irreversible act to embed them in a printed text. Suiko may be seen as an aesthetic that arises from this awareness. And there in the background, behind the desire for perfection and sophistication, lies the receptive power of the color white.

During my childhood, I learned my characters by writing them

Chapter 4

Back to White

sarily inflating the impression of meaning. Silence, when used effectively, actually secures meaning; it is a necessary part of communication, and wisdom.

The roots of expressions like "Simple is Best," and "Less is More" are subtly different than those that underlie emptiness. Emptiness does not merely imply simplicity of form, logical sophistication, and the like. Rather, emptiness provides a space within which our imaginations can run free, vastly enriching our powers of perception and our mutual comprehension. Emptiness is this potential. Therefore, even if someone self-consciously applies a simple geometric style to his work, or maintains a pretentious silence, he or she cannot grasp the true meaning of emptiness. One must train oneself and build up experience in order to apply that concept efficiently. The ideal that we strive for is the realization of a plan that will evoke the imaginative powers of our audience.

Creativity and "questioning" are made of the same stuff. A creative question is a form of expression – it requires no definite answer. That is because it holds countless answers within itself.

begins at ground zero; rather, I believe that they stem from our unconscious impulse to "inquire." To "inquire" is predicated on "I think" – it establishes that emptiness that sets our brains to work.

The following example is not perfect, but it may help me explain the relationship of emptiness to thought. There is a rather unusual Japanese noodle dish called *wanko soba*. One is served a small amount of noodles, which one proceeds to slurp down. As soon as one is finished, the waitress brings a second serving. If the customer downs these noodles as well, another batch is served immediately. Because the quantity of *soba* is small enough to be consumed in a single gulp, this cycle of serving and eating repeats itself numerous times. The customer cannot easily control his eating speed, since he must follow the brisk rhythm created by the waitress. Whenever she brings another serving of noodles, she pours the noodles into his bowl and adds the empty serving bowl to the stack in front of him, so the bowls pile higher and higher. Customers may take this as a challenge to eat more than the others in the restaurant, or at least feel some sense of achievement watching the pile grow, so they continue eating. The mounting pile of bowls seems like proof of their accomplishment.

The act of thinking is a lot like a reversal of the process of eating *wanko soba*. In short, the customer looks at the empty bowls piled up before his eyes and fills them with his "thoughts" rather than with "noodles." He follows a certain rhythm when he does this; first one thought fills a bowl, then, in a flash, another, then another . . . In this manner, like a conditioned reflex, "thought" accumulates before our eyes. I have no idea of the exact path our thoughts take, but the example of the empty noodle bowls reflects the general mechanism. In short, our brains automatically insert "answers" into small empty spaces. In this fashion, emptiness carries our thinking process forward.

Creative Questions Require no Answers

"Silence is eloquent." This phrase may sound contradictory, but at this point in my discussion, its repercussions should be understandable in concrete terms. Garrulity causes the value of words to deteriorate by unneces-

The following are Sen no Rikyu's "Seven Rules for the Way of Tea":

> Arrange flowers as if they are growing in the field
> Lay the charcoal so that it heats the water well
> In the summer, suggest coolness
> In the winter, warmth
> Be ready ahead of time
> Prepare for rain just in case
> Treat guests with the utmost consideration

You may wonder, 'is that all?' Yet countless metaphorical possibilities are suggested in these words. For example, "as if they are growing in the field" draws one's attention to the fact that a flower arrangement must appear natural; yet how can such a state be reached through artificial means – one is bound to fail, however much effort one puts in! If we interpret this Rule more broadly, so as to include all living things and the seasons, however, then the problem of how to do things "naturally" – in short, the thorny question of consciousness – reverberates on a much wider scale.

Although the tea ceremony consists of the simple act of serving and drinking tea, the whole activity can be taken as a metaphor. Rikyu's Seven Rules imply various aspects of human activity, all of which reflect the concept of emptiness. In other words, the rules form a resource for the tea ceremony, enabling a person to communicate with people and objects. And the principle of emptiness functions within these rules.

Thought Dwells in Emptiness

To this point, I have used the concept of emptiness to help explain how we communicate in various ways by trying to creatively understand each other's intentions. Emptiness is a part of this process of communication, since our brains move to fill in that which is missing. In other words, communication and ideas emerge from emptiness. Mental activities like "pondering" and "ideating" do not emerge from a conscious process of "thinking" that

refined structure of the ceremony encourages one to serve the tea with the utmost sincerity.

When a host invites his guest into his tiny tea house for an exchange of thoughts, there is a reason for the scant furnishings: one's imagination expands in uncluttered, simple space. The host's own unique taste is expressed through the flower arrangement and the scroll painting on the wall of the alcove, both of which change with the occasion and the season. For example, a basin filled with water and floating flower petals allow the host and his guest to imagine themselves sitting together under a blossoming cherry tree. The act of interpreting the meaning of the display to develop and expand on the underlying messages it conveys is called *mitate*. Since the humble space contains few concrete objects, our imaginations are freed – we can imagine the room under a cherry tree in full bloom, on a quiet seashore listening to the waves, or at the bottom of a well.

There is an anecdote that Sen no Rikyu picked and threw away all the morning glories he had in his garden to receive Hideyoshi (1536-1598), one of the most powerful warlords in Japan, with only a single morning glory flower on the tea house floor. The tea house's very emptiness turns it into a stage, on which human consciousness can rise to the metaphysical level.

Perhaps the polar opposite of the theatrical approach embodied in Rikyu's tea house can be found in genres like the opera or the musical. Operas and musicals enrich imagination and stimulate the senses directly through effects like the portrayal of reality, the exaggeration of corporeal beauty, lighting and music. Rikyu's tea house rejects these decorative features to evoke illusion and fantasy through extremely limited effects and actions.

The garden path leading to the tea house is a transitional space; one walks from the realm of the mundane to enter the world of the sacred. As one passes through the scrupulously trimmed natural space, one's perceptions become more acute. As a result, one's five senses are sharpened to an extent where he is not affected by any external changes; and he carries his purified senses to the tiny hut and sits on the floor. Accordingly, the senses as "information" become a rich source of imagination in the tea house.

corridor, and the white light bursting through the paper sliding doors together form one of the original motifs of spatial construction in Japan. With *fusuma*; screen partitions making up two sides of the room, we can see the basic layout of what today is called the Japanese-style room, or *washitsu*.

In this simple, pure space, the original prototype of the tea house, Yoshimasa savored his tea and let his mind flow in tranquility.

The founder of the simple tea ceremony (*wabicha*), Shuko (1423-1502), must have conversed with Yoshimasa many times in this room. Shuko abandoned his taste for foreign luxuries, and discovered beauty in the austere and the withered, or so-called *wabi*. One can only imagine how Shuko and Yoshimasa spent their time in the *Dojinsai* of the Silver Temple's, and what new ideas they exchanged there.

Takeno Jo-o (1502-1555) inherited Shuko's tea ceremony and made it more "Japanese," striving to use ever more simple forms to reach people's inner selves and complex thoughts. Simplicity leads to emptiness, the space where people's minds reside – as we have seen, it is the origin of communication, and reflected in things like Japanese myth. A teaspoon is a simple object, whose only significant feature is its bamboo joint. Until the invention of the bamboo spoon by Jo-o, elaborately patterned imported ivory spoons were used in the tea ceremony; from this difference we can clearly understand how this sort of move towards simplicity was the origin of his "Japanese style."

Soon, tea ceremony techniques and utensils, as well as the shape of the tea house, were established under the guidance of another tea master, Sen no Rikyu (1522-1591). Simplicity and tranquility were paramount in his creative approach. Because the objects he used are simple, they lead us to imagine things through our senses. They are receptive in their communicative power, as well as in the countless ideas they inspire. This simplicity is both the conceptual basis and the ideal of the tea ceremony.

The tea house shrank during Rikyu's time, while the ceremony became casual and nonchalant; yet despite the outward simplicity, the atmosphere was filled with intense energy. The tea canister, the cups, and the flower arrangement were all extremely simple. When one offers tea to a guest, one must follow the ritual sequence with an earnest heart; and the

treasures during the Onin War was far more devastating than can be imagined today. In the end, Yoshimasa relinquished his position as Shogun to his son and retired to Higashiyama, the range of low mountains along Kyoto's eastern border.

The *Jishoji* temple, better known today as *Ginkaku* (the Temple of the Silver Pavilion, or Silver Temple for short), is the villa Yoshimasa built in Higashiyama. He passed his time there peacefully immersed in calligraphy and painting, and performing the tea ceremony. In retrospect, he can be seen as a central figure in the creation of a new type of culture that took the name of the place where he lived, Higashiyama. In short, one era had been brought to a close by the Onin War, and another had begun with the emergence of Higashiyama culture.

Why did Higashiyama aesthetics put such an emphasis on "simplicity," or "emptiness"? Could a general war-weariness have caused Yoshimasa and his fellow Kyotoites to look at the world differently? Perhaps. What is more important than such idle guesswork is the fact that Japanese desperately sought beauty in simplicity on their own from this period on, breaking away from foreign influences.

The Origins of the Japanese-style Room

There is a beautiful room in one corner of the Silver Temple marked by a perfectly balanced tension. This is the *Togudo*, the study where the retired shogun spent most of his time. *Tatami* mats there were not placed on only one part of the floor, as was the custom then, but spread throughout the room. The *Dojinsai* is a square-shaped room of four and a half mats, covering an area of about seven square meters.

A raised *chodai* is placed in the room for writing, and the wall next to it consists of *shoji*; a pair of sliding paper screen doors that function as a window. When one slides the doors open, the garden is right before his eyes. There are *chigaidana*; shelves on the left side of the *chodai*, which were probably used for things like books or decorative objects. On the right side of the *chodai*, there is another pair of sliding doors connected to the corridor. The shadow cast by the extending eaves, the deep shadows that fill the

symbols of the power to control.

Human beings are social animals, who pursue their lives as part of a collectivity. From the very beginning of human history, therefore, designs applied to tools and instruments were expressive of power relationships in the communities that produced them. Accordingly, we can never find bronze vessels that are simple and unadorned – they always have densely decorated surfaces with detailed patterns. A similar logic underlies the dragon motif in China, geometric designs in Islam, and the detailed elaborations of the Baroque and Rococo styles; they represent the majesty of their rulers, and the ascendance of their national cultures.

It has been just a century and a half since people discovered the practicality of simple objects and became aware of their beauty and value. The collapse of absolute power brought about a new type of society, "civil society," where individuals could freely choose a means to live, a place to dwell, and jobs. As this "modern" society formed, a new stress was placed on the practicality of the simple and the minimal. At the same time, modern individuals started to create their own environment, and their sense of beauty and value became based on the idea of practicality, and the maximization of resources. We can understand the logic of practicality within this historical context.

Nevertheless, it was at the middle of the Muromachi period, which preceded European modernism by several centuries, that Japan discovered the value of simplicity. How can we explain the birth of this aesthetic in Japan?

Perhaps we should begin with the Muromachi Shogun, Ashikaga Yoshimasa (1436 - 1490), a cultivated man with a keen sense of beauty. Yoshimasa was doubtlessly affected by the wide-scale loss of cultural artifacts burnt during the Onin War (1467-1477), events which he himself had been deeply involved in. How pained he must have been to witness the civilization that had been nurtured in Kyoto since ancient times turned to ashes because of man's foolish desires. Shrines and temples representing generations of skilled craftsmanship, paper scrolls filled with dazzling colors, the marvelous brushwork produced by great artists of the past, long-standing religious and aesthetic beliefs – all had vanished. In fact, the loss of cultural

ness in Japan naturally drew my attention to Higashiyama (Eastern Mountain) culture at the middle of the Muromachi period. An aesthetic of emptiness in the tea ceremony was formed between mid Muromachi and the Momoyama period. The theme of this book is white, which makes it tricky to know how far to go in delineating the power of emptiness. Yet white (白) and emptiness (空) are closely intertwined. The concept of empty space (空白) brings these two things together. There is "emptiness" in white, and there is also "white' in emptiness. It is my hope that readers can grasp the concept of white by examining how the concept of emptiness is reflected in the tea ceremony.

The Tea Ceremony

Tea utensils are beautiful in their simplicity. The tea canister I keep on hand is coated with the liquid from the Japanese lacquer tree; the glow emitted by its finely curved surface is composed of the reflections of all the shades of light around it, as if it were filled to the brim with water. The delicate shape of the long, narrow spoon used to scoop out the tea also never fails to draw my attention. Its structural accent is simplicity, as if its bamboo joint had just been cut in the grove; its finely crafted beauty comes from the balanced tension between nature and consciousness.

  Why is simplicity so powerful and inspiring? I would like to investigate this matter in relation to a Japanese sensibility that has derived from the discovery of simple beauty.

  In ancient time, people found beauty in ornamental details which endowed objects with meaning or power. From the Bronze Age to the birth of absolute monarchy during the Jomon Period in Japan, and throughout most of the cultural histories of China, Europe, Islam, and Esoteric Buddhism, human beings have celebrated power by placing complicated patterns on objects.

  It was through this clear display of collective power embodied in elaborate patterns that unity among people and between nations could be symbolically expressed. The craftsmen who did the work required extensive training as well as time, and their ornamental works were highly valued as

is seen as peace. I would like to reiterate, however, that the red circle by itself creates no meaning, only interpretation.

The symbolism of a fluttering white flag with a red disc in the center functions independently, regardless of how people think of it. The Olympic banner, for example, generates a powerful centripetal force when it's raised, because it reflects the ideas and thoughts of people all over the world. This is the power of communication attached to the symbol.

Accordingly, the power of a symbol goes in tandem with its receptiveness. Because the simple and abstract quality of red circle on white background is so equivocal, it can be filled with various images. Its composition is one case where a figure signifies something only in its relation to the background. In other words, the circle appears red when contrasted with white; and its shape is circular in its relation to the rectangular background. I previously discussed the significance of the four colors – red, black, white, and blue – in Japanese culture, and here, in this example, the contrast of red and white is maximized. A burning red is placed on a shining white, which commemorates the bright and the dark, clarity and dimness.

There aren't many symbols that possess such great receptivity. Perhaps the symbol of Christianity, the cross, is another good example in terms of its power to focus the mind.

Symbols' receptivity makes them attract attention, and they can represent innumerable meanings. There is no right or wrong reading of a symbol. There may be different levels of receptiveness for a symbol in terms of its functionality; yet, since the symbol itself is empty to begin with, it can be neither evil nor good. If there is one aspect that might be seen as important, it is how its latent power is applied in a given situation. Therefore, even if our flag inevitably reflects a sad history, it can still hold every possible meaning if we place our will and hope in it. The Japanese flag fulfills its function silently while embracing the contradictory notions of sadness, disgrace, hope, and peace.

Emptiness and White

My investigation of the origins of the conscious use of the concept of empti-

used to smoothly reach an agreement. This communication mechanism may appear illogical when cunning politicians abuse it to avoid their responsibilities; but its essential nature is actually very logical indeed.

We need traffic signs that clearly differentiate between "stop" and "go" at traffic intersections. If we look at a circular road junction like a "roundabout," however, drivers can move forward to their desired positions without stopping. Of course, this is not a perfect comparison, but removing a crucial issue from discussion as a communication technique is like a skillful elimination of traffic signs from an intersection. When a central issue is bracketed, there may be some confusion as to what should be inserted there; however, such confusion and misunderstanding can be seen as another aspect of this technique. The national flag of Japan can be used to illustrate this point.

The Receptiveness of a Red Circle on a White Background

The national flag of Japan is white with a red disk in the center. We can say that the flag is a symbol that exemplifies the meaning of emptiness.

The red circle has no meaning. It is simply a red circle, and nothing beyond that. To give it a meaning such as nation, the Japanese emperor, or patriotism, is purely arbitrary. The fact that the red circle grabs our attention makes it an effective means of communicating and circulating whatever special meaning is used to fill it. Since it is initially empty, any meaning will do, whether it be invasion, destruction and imperialism, or patriotism and peace. Because I am of the postwar generation, I learned at school that the circle symbolizes a peaceful nation. I might create a big stir in the classroom if I mentioned this at a Chinese university; and I understand that there are people for whom such an interpretation would necessarily be painful. There was a fixed content in the so-called red circle for the countless soldiers who placed the flag on their foreheads and then went out and killed and died during World War II. Yet the relationship between sign and meaning is arbitrary. You are basically free to interpret the circle as you wish; it could signify the sun in Shinto, or sincerity, or a pickled plum in a bed of rice. To those who were taught that the meaning of the circle was peace, it

pared to the western system, which features clearly indicated subjects in logically constructed sentences. However, communication techniques like *a-un no kokyu*, *nemawashi*, and *haragei* are in fact highly refined. Since subjects are often left unclear, it becomes impossible to point out who is specifically responsible for a given statement. Rather, the Japanese system is one of forming consensus by settling things in silence. Reaching a public consensus through this system is a highly developed form of collective communication; and it is natural for people to acknowledge that the way they reached a mutual agreement is satisfying. Perhaps one could study collective communication on the Net today through a close analysis of this kind of consensus method.

When people are making an extremely important decision, they don't express the issue or its objective directly; instead, they bracket the matter through an application of emptiness in communication. The essential structure of a conversation of this sort runs as follows:

> "May (　) proceed (　) in such (　) a way?"
> The group remains silent.
> "Since there are no objections, it has been decided to proceed (　) that (　) way."

Clearly, this system is extremely difficult for non-Japanese to fathom. An issue may be pressing but it is not directly declared as a noun; rather it is replaced by an impersonal pronoun in order to effectively hold the matter back. No particular person makes the decision by himself, but those present, as participants, share the responsibility for the decision equally, their silence being understood as a sign of approval. Here, the pronoun signifies the topic, filling it with content as if filling an empty vessel. It doesn't mean that the matter has been adjusted or moderated to dispel the ambiguity. Instead it is a concrete application of emptiness among the concerned parties who clearly understand the statement and move to reach a consensus without resorting to the exercise of individual responsibility or power. The crucial point is not buried underneath the silence; rather it attains flexibility in emptiness so that it structurally supports the procedure

other application of the concept of emptiness expressed through white. It is a very old tradition from this ancient religion; and at the same time, it is a form of human environment, of so-called design. The core of communication in Japanese culture is "emptiness," which exists together with that concept called "white."

Nothing is Said

Communication is commonly assumed to involve a meaningful linguistic exchange of some sort, yet there are times when words and content are unnecessary: eye contact, for example, can be a very effective way of sharing thoughts and ideas. It may not always be appropriate to deliver information in this fashion; yet if both sides exchange their thoughts through their eyes, it can be understood as a successful communication. What we call communication is a mechanism of transmission that effectively guides content – i.e. a comprehensible piece of information – through a medium. Yet communication doesn't start and end with a mere exchange of signs. If both sides signal their agreement by nodding their heads simultaneously, a bond is established between them. Should such an understanding be completed through eye contact alone, intentionally avoiding the encoding and decoding of signs, it can be considered the best communication possible. Japanese people call this ideal condition "a breath of alpha and omega" (*a-un no kokyu*). A pair of stone-carved guardian dogs is placed at the entrance of Shinto shrines; the one on the left exhales "*a*" while the other inhales "*un*." In terms of communication, this can be described as a process of sending and receiving. When this exchanging process is performed simultaneously, an instant and mutual understanding occurs; this is the "*a-un*" moment.

The Japanese system of communication is often criticized as difficult to understand. Leaving so much unsaid can make a discussion appear ambiguous. The subject of a sentence, for example, is often dropped. Moreover, Japanese people tend to leave unclear matters as they are in discussion by using such techniques as *nemawashi* (a delicate and often painstaking process of consensus-building) and *haragei* (the implicit signaling of one's intentions). These approaches may appear difficult to comprehend com-

next to the previously established building, so that two buildings, one old and one new, stand side by side once every twenty years. More than a thousand pieces of ritual implements are replaced with entirely new ones, and these objects find their places in the new building. Thus the old building is terminated through a process of deconstruction.

The blueprint of the shrine also changes every 20 years, during the rebuilding process. No attempt is made to preserve the preceding plan – rather, it is reformulated through the act of re-drafting. Physical differences naturally occur during this process, but the key issues are the fresh ideas and sensitivities which attach themselves to the refinement of the draft. Through reproduction, information is transformed into a new life form.

Construction methods are similarly handed down by succeeding generations of shrine carpenters. A new master carpenter takes charge of the rebuilding after completed his training under the previous master builder. At the time when a new *yashiro*'s pillars are raised, the master chants a spell; this does not carry any specific meaning, but has been passed down as an oral ritual that must be accurately transmitted and performed.

Shrine architecture has been passed down though these changing blueprints and generations of shrine carpenters for more than a thousand years; gradually shifting from its original form into a shape that embodies Japanese sensitivity. The Japanese people have accomplished the move from Polynesian style architecture to a clean-cut simplicity through a process of transformation which mirrors the process by which life forms evolve, passing down both the original as well as newly acquired information, encoded in DNA, to the next generation.

In the previous chapter, I mentioned that white is information emerging from chaos, activity surrounding the rebuilding of the Ise Shrine is a ritual of rebirth that brings form to chaos, then pulls it back again as new through a device we could call the transmission of techniques. We may say that *zotai* is an attempt to restore the shrine as information; it is the *itoshiroshiki* that has passed through chaos. Through this process, the already "familiar" object is purified and transformed into a new "unknown" entity. A *yashiro* newly built with white cypress is divinely white.

The shrine attendants perform their daily ritual in white attire, an-

and finally release their mind while facing the center of *yashiro*. Because the basic principle of the *yashiro* is its emptiness, it functions as a vessel to receive people's thoughts and wishes. The center of the empty space is not a place to send off messages to the gods; its role is to embrace people's earnest desires as if it were a vessel to be filled. An empty offering box is placed in the shrine; and people put money and their wishes together in it. The Shinto shrine serves to link humans and gods, fulfilling its role through maintaining its emptiness. At the same time, people seek peace through emptying their minds there, in anticipation of a god's possible visit.

Information and the Ise Shrine

Shinto's most holy site, the Ise shrine to the Sun Goddess, seems to have a complicated structure, yet its principle is as simple as that of the *yashiro*: it holds empty space in the center and represents its power in terms of the chance of becoming. The "non-color" white, as a symbol of emptiness, plays a role in this. Zig-zag strips of white paper hang from sacred straw festoons on the four pillars; the passage leading towards the shrine is covered with white pebbles; and the boundary between the world of gods and the secular world is divided by a square of white cloth. When it flutters in the wind, the white cloth signifies communication between the two worlds, as if some living thing were passing through it.

It seems that the Ise shrine was influenced by South Polynesian architecture. It is commonly believed that Roman culture arrived in China through the Silk Road, and that Japan received it via China and Korea. However, the Japanese archipelago is positioned facing the southern part of Asia, and connected to this world through the ocean. Thanks to this geographical location, Japanese culture has been influenced by cultures from all over the world. Although the architecture of the Ise shrine has clear Pacific and Polynesian features, however, Japan has tirelessly refined these over the ages, transforming it into a purely Japanese artifact.

The Ise shrine is completely rebuilt once every 20 years, a process called *shikinen zotai*, or *zotai* for short. In other words, the life span of this particular *yashiro* is set at 20 years. Each successive structure is erected

Shinto's "eight million gods" are not merely localized deities but exist universally. They float above village houses and silently hover over oceans or rivers. There are gods flying between the trees in the forest, and in radishes freshly pulled from the earth. A rice grain hosts seven gods. Gods inhabit freshly drawn water, and even decomposed objects. People cannot "kidnap" gods, who exist freely in nature, for their own benefit – the idea is unthinkable. However, they can establish an "empty space" which will catch the gods' attention as a place they "may" enter whenever they please.

A Shinto shrine, adorned with the natural objects used in ritual, is where the gods are welcomed; the knots atop the four pillars signal that the space has been completed. The act of placing one's hands together in concentrated prayer before this possibility – in other words, Shinto – was established in this spot specifically designed to attract those wandering deities who "might" enter.

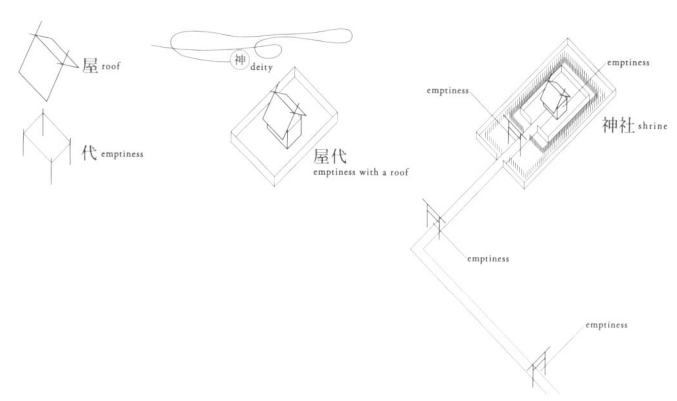

屋 roof
代 emptiness
神 deity
屋代 emptiness with a roof
神社 shrine
emptiness

Yashiro, the central empty space that sits like a carport between the tasseled poles, simply means *shiro* with a roof. The Shinto shrine of today, though, has a more elaborate layout, with a distinctive gate (*torii*), a passage that leads to the shrine, and fencing around the *yashiro* to clarify and delineate its borders. People worship at a shrine by following a sequence of actions; they pass through the archway, reach the shrine, clap their hands,

"Pine Trees" is one of the prototypes that shape and convey this aesthetic taste. As *The Collection of Painting Techniques*, produced in the Edo period, says: "When construed as part of a larger pattern, even white paper can be satisfying." In other words, an unpainted space should not be seen as an information-free area: the foundation of Japanese aesthetics lies in that empty space, and a host of meanings have been built upon it. An important level of communication thus exists within the dimension we call "white."

Emptiness as Limitless Potential

An empty state possesses a chance of becoming by virtue of its receptive nature. The mechanism of communication is activated when we look at an empty vessel, not as a negative state, but in terms of its capability to be filled with something. The ancient Japanese religion of Shinto worships the "eight million gods" within nature, but when we look at it from a different angle, we can understand it as a technique of communication, an imaginative power that invites wandering gods from everywhere. How, then, is empty space constructed in Shinto architecture?

A Shinto shrine, (*jinja*), is a central space hosting people's religious activities. It is also called *shiro*, or *yashiro*; and its basic principle is "to embrace emptiness." In its original form, four pillars were raised on the ground and their tops tied with sacred ropes, leaving an "empty space" in the center. Precisely because this space is designed to be "empty," there is always the possibility that something may enter it. This "may" too is crucial – it can be seen as the essence of Shinto, the thing that activates people's minds and leads them to prayer.

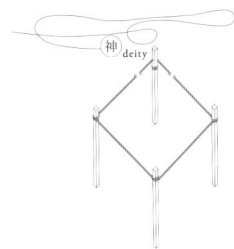

free on paper was the crowning achievement of Southern Sung paintings. Not surprisingly, Tohaku's painting bears some similarity to that of the Southern Sung painter, Mokkei (Muqi, 1210-1269). Tohaku's provocative demonstration of empty space and emptiness is crystallized in "Pine Trees." It conveys the lively image of the trees by intentionally avoiding detailed description, an approach that activates the imaginations of its viewers. In short, the painting's very roughness and omission of details awakens our senses.

Haboku is one of the ink painting techniques connected to this swift and harsh movement of the brush. *Haboku* is meant to enable viewers to imagine the landscape within an ever-changing nature; in short, it aims to help them expand their imaginations. Tohaku's screen painting is a prime example of how such images are constructed.

Second, Tohaku's "Pine Trees" seems to emphasize the empty space between the trees rather than the trees themselves. Perhaps we should say that the painstaking execution of the misty atmosphere is the main theme of the painting rather than the trees themselves. The pines look indistinct, being fused into the depth of whiteness. Far from signifying a state of non-being, the white empty space suggests the countless trees that stand behind the painted surface. The exquisitely dense atmosphere is filled with a subtle movement that leaves viewers' senses drifting in that space. The painting's most important feature is the way its mists evoke the boundless, floating world of the imagination.

A sacred mountain is painted in white on the screen to the left, taking up two sections on its upper right-hand portion; the feeling of distance is created by the use of the whitest white. It is left as empty space on the painted surface; yet it could also be said that the mountain is hidden behind the white mist. Here, the surrounding scenery, from the nearest to the most distant view, lies buried in the hazy ground. Despite its vagueness, our senses are drawn into that white space, where they are left to sway back and forth.

Japanese people have a high regard for this paradoxical expression of empty space in pictorial art; and it has helped them develop an imaginative capability that moves far beyond natural descriptive detail. Tohaku's

The Meaning of Emptiness

In some cases, white denotes "emptiness." White as non-color transforms into a symbol of non-being. Yet emptiness doesn't mean "nothingness" or "energy-less"; rather, in many cases, it indicates a condition, or *kizen*, which will likely be filled with content in the future. On the basis of this assumption, the application of white is able to create a forceful energy for communication.

A creative mind, in short, does not see an empty bowl as valueless, but perceives it as existing in a transitional state, waiting for the content that will eventually fill it; and this creative perspective instills power in the emptiness. The deep relationship between *kuhaku*, or "emptiness," and the color white is established through this communicative process.

Hasegawa Tohaku's "Pine Trees"

Hasegawa Tohaku's (1539-1610) screen painting, "Pine Trees," is one of Japan's most celebrated art works. It consists of a pair of six-fold screens, two six-piece paintings symmetrically positioned side by side, painted with powerful, dynamic brush strokes. In this work, we can find highly diverse yet always effective applications of white and emptiness.

First, the pine grove is constructed using a rough, even harsh brush technique, a manner of representing the real world that makes the trees seem more "real." This monotone painting gives the impression that the pine trees are depicted in much greater detail than is actually the case.

"Pine Trees" inherited the legacy of the Southern Sung ink painting tradition, the quintessence of Chinese fine art. Chinese ink painting reached its peak during the Sung period, an achievement that can be compared to that of the European Renaissance. We can classify Sung painting into two; the Northern Sung style and the Southern Sung style. Unlike the detailed descriptions of nature found in Northern Sung painting, the Southern Sung style delineates the boundlessness of empty space by blending the "subtle" and the "faint" together while avoiding portraying structural forms in any detail. The technique of using emptiness to set the image

Chapter 3

Emptiness

way. Through this casting process, western technology introduced a newly systemized typography in China for missionary purposes. Japan came into contact with this new print technology through this route as well.

Despite the cultural boundary between East and West, and the technological gap dividing those civilizations, the sense of beauty attached to typeface has been cultivated through the simple act of placing characters on paper. In this regard, Guttenberg's cast type and Chinese woodcut printing share a common feature. Letters became independent objects through the sheer fact of being printed in black on white paper.

Both the Gothic style of alphabet letters and the *kaishu* standard of Chinese characters have been passed down and filtered through the principle of legibility; capturing our attention with their refinement. Indeed, from the inscriptions on ancient Chinese oracle bones to the completion of the Ming font, from the chisel work on old Roman marbles to the perfection of that delicate curve that embodies the balance of the universe, the history of workmanship and practice is unimaginably long. The letters we see on paper today have passed along that long channel of history; through meditating on their development, our imagination deepens.

efficient. Yet it didn't reach maturity because it was technically difficult and inefficient to mold tens of thousands of highly complicated characters. Furthermore, people's aesthetic preferences slowed the advance of the technology compared to the West; the Chinese preferred the precise and detailed woodcuts to the dull-looking characters the metal and ceramic typesets turned out.

What is commonly understood as the standard Chinese writing style, the so-called *kaishu*, emerged much later than the cursive and grass styles. In other words, it was not the decline of *kaishu* that led to the appearance of the cursive and grass styles. The oldest calligraphic, *Xiao Zhuan*, refers to the seal script (*zhuan shu*) and the clerical script (*lishu*), standardized by the Emperor Qin Shi Huang (259-210 BC). In this style, emphasis was placed on the pictorial depiction of the characters as a whole rather than the delineation of each separate point and stroke. After a long period of modification, it was finally established as *kaishu* by the prominent calligrapher, Qu Yang Sun (557-641 AD). During the Sung dynasty, *kaishu* was the standard for both woodcut printing and ceramic typesets.

The typographic structure of *kaishu* is thus referred to as "Sung font," and recognized as one of the most elegant calligraphic styles in the history of East Asian printing. During the later Qing (1644-1912) dynasty, though, it was re-standardized, once again attaining that abstract quality we find in the Kang Xi dictionary, until it finally evolved into the "Ming font" we see today.

The distinctively pointy ends of the strokes in the Ming font characters, the so-called *uroko* ("fish scale" in Japanese), are meant to represent the beginnings and ends of brush strokes; a form that was supposedly retained in order to maximize the legibility and structural composition of characters on paper.

The metal cast type form of printing technology was introduced to China at the end of the Qing dynasty by westerners, specifically Christian missionaries who came to East Asia to proselytize. The structural shape of the Ming font resembles a particular European typography, the so-called Bodoni; a similarity which, it is assumed, derived from the background of the missionaries, which led them to interpret the Ming style in a certain

uted to the printing of portable manuals. As these examples illustrate, the development of typography flourished in late 15th century Venice, and required a good balance between form and intelligence. The art was refined and polished in Europe, the product of countless trials and errors at the juncture of culture and technology.

Roman style
Garamond Regular

Ming font
Ryumin H-KL

Letters were formed over a long passage of time.

Soon, typography was caught up in the modern art movement, a new historical wave that aimed to deconstruct forms of the past completely and reconstruct them according to new aesthetic standards. In the process, the hallmark of Roman style, *serif*, was sucked under. The result was a new style, the so-called *sans-serif* (without *serif*) which replaced its predecessor. In mid-20th century Switzerland, a new era of typography was launched by the typefaces created by people like Max Miedinger (1910-1980), who raised the status of modern typography through his masterpiece of *sans-serif*, the "Helvetica," and Adrian Frutiger (1928-), who categorized the weight and proportion of characters, and integrated them according to his design, which he called "Univers" (universe). From these Swiss origins arose a foundation for perfecting calligraphic styles, and establishing a total system of characters. Although the development of printing was shaped by the history of ideas and technology, it was this driving passion for beauty that made books what they are today.

In China, ceramic typeface was invented by Pi Sheng (990-1051) in the 11th century, during the Sung dynasty; the beautifully executed square script he developed preceded Guttenberg by a full 400 years. At that time, carving characters on wooden panels – so-called woodcut printing – was already common practice, so the ceramic typeface was intended to be more

the literary domain. Unlike men, whose solid Chinese characters reflected their higher social status, *hiragana* conveyed a subtle world of fine emotion in grass-like lines that seemed to dance across the Japanese paper (*washi*). In this way, the stylized technique of writing in *hiragana* led to the creation of a new aesthetic separate and distinct from textual "meaning."

The purpose of this book is not to compile examples from eastern and western cultures in this manner. Rather, I want to verify that characters as a "form" within a flat, square surface constituted a fully developed aesthetic that transcended their linguistic use. Paper's seductive power led to the steady growth of knowledge, quickly joined by a new sense of beauty. In short, paper evolved into a medium that recorded and preserved both intellectual and aesthetic achievement. It thus seems especially worthwhile today to invest at least a little energy into examining the cultural tapestry of that seemingly endless stretch of time we call the Middle Ages.

Typeface and Typography

The invention of movable type revolutionized the reproduction and circulation of information; yet at the same time its decorative inscriptions raised the curtain on a new aesthetic. The objective of Gutenberg's press was to widely circulate the Bible. Unlike the electronic media today, typesets were not formalized on a practical basis, and the typeface was inspired by the soaring Gothic style. This style marked the initial stage of the Gutenberg text, the so-called *incunabula*, which seems to have stood against the authority and the dignity of handwritten texts; yet there was a hidden motivation behind this new standard. Black inked letters stamped on paper created a different flavor and texture compared to handwriting. People will always find beauty wherever possible, and thus could hardly fail to recognize their latent beauty. From this point on, numerous typeface designers poured their passion into refining this beauty, a passion that manifested itself in the domain of typography.

In the case of alphabet typography, Nicholas Jenson's (1420-1480) outstanding achievement was the multi-purpose, highly legible "Roman-style"; while Aldus Manitius (1449-1515) created "Italic," which contrib-

even in the East Asian "kanji" cultural sphere. If we look at books as a medium whose main function is to store letters, then perhaps the factors underlying this trend are practicality and efficiency.

On Letters

Whatever form characters or letters may take, however they may be laid out – in short, whatever sense of beauty they may add to a book – the prime motive behind their birth is not mere practicality. Although each character is part of a language system, it was also created as an aesthetic object.

In Roman times, the alphabet was usually carved on stone using sharp tools, so as a result the Roman script has a raised flourish – a "serif" – at the end of each stroke. This can be seen as a visual manifestation of people's appreciation of letters' beauty. Since the carved words were deeply associated with politics and religion, a powerful aura radiated from the delicate structure of letters and their combinations. In short, they were far more than words to be read – their grand and magnificent inscriptions affected the course of human destiny. Even today we bow before the overwhelming power and majestic beauty of the Magna Charta parchment. The "dignity" embedded in its densely marshaled letters represents the authority of the handwritten text.

The profundity of the scriptures, poetry, and Zen Buddhist language which we find in East Asian calligraphy, a supreme example of the fluid grace of black ink on white paper, gave the world of written expression – as opposed to the spoken language – a new maturity. The use of the brush came to flourish relatively early in China, so that even the carved characters on stone show calligraphic features. The purposes behind these features extended beyond linguistic boundaries.

Of course characters can invoke awe by instilling a sense of dignity and authority, but they can also undermine authority gently and softly by touching people's delicate emotions. *Hiragana*, a cursive syllabary devised over a thousand years ago in the Heian Period, conveyed a sense of beauty that naturally deconstructed the authoritative, didactic status of *kanji*. By using *hiragana* exclusively, Heian women were able to play an active role in

object into two pieces using our two hands, we get a straight line, while a second break results in a right angle. Another possibility comes from the nature of gravity, which turns a hanging vine or string into a straight vertical line. We could speculate endlessly on such possibilities, but the fact remains that when sheepskins were turned into writing materials, they were always cut into rectangles. This process may be understood as one of the origins of design.

Correspondingly, paper today is manufactured in the form of a roll, which is then cut into sheets that have a ratio of $1:\sqrt{2}$. If we cut the sheet in half and then cut it in half a second time, this ratio stays the same – the proportional relationship between length and width remains constant. TV screens and computer monitors are rectangular but stretch sideways, reflecting the horizontal placement of our eyes.

Books are made of rectangular sheets of paper. Can we not say then that language is folded and stored in rectangular space? Basically speaking, language appears in linear form. Humans cannot utter more than a single word at a time; were that possible, communication would be even more complex than it is. When we speak, we are solo instruments. This linear structure remains the rule when our language is arranged in letters. A book is a vessel constructed through controlling this unbroken string of language, folded into a defined space. While the western alphabet is written horizontally, from left to right, characters in the East Asian cultural sphere are written vertically, from top to bottom. Except for things like "cursive" or "grass-style" calligraphy and certain stylized scripts, letters or characters are treated as movable atomic particles – whether they are hieroglyphs representing shapes, or phonograms representing sound, they can be freely aligned in any direction. Phoenician characters, the ancient predecessors of the alphabet, were initially written from right to left, but at some point they started being written from left to right. This may have something to do with the advent of ox-drawn plows, whose furrows followed a similar pattern.

Whether symbols were printed on wooden or bamboo strips, or on parchment, the left to right or top to bottom structure was established naturally, perhaps because writing tools were usually held in the right hand. Today, horizontal writing that runs left to right is gradually taking over,

er still. We can say that this series of whites is highly conceptualized, but if we think of white as sensual experience, then the poem brings us closer to white's essential quality. Furthermore, picturing white as a square makes its whiteness all the more striking. Perhaps for this reason, this image resembles the concrete process of papermaking. The liquid in the vat is white, and one scoops it up to make sheets of paper that appear even more white. Each, though, seems whiter than the sheet that came before it. This repetitive process of producing white continues on and on. The poem captures this scooping process, like a turning flywheel that gives birth to life.

Folding Language

Books are repositories of human wisdom in linguistic form, and they have seen many improvements since their inception. Methods of printing have been evolved to store the wisdom and technology, aesthetics and thought, that are contained within them in the form of clearly delineated text.

Before the invention of paper, thin layers of tanned sheepskin – called vellum or parchment – were used as printing material in Europe and the Near East. Ancient Egyptians used another material, papyrus, which was made from vertically sliced plant stems that were pressed and then dried. In China, characters were written on wooden or bamboo strips, which were tied together with string to form a sheet. In all of these cases, the final product took the form of a rectangle, even though the contours of dried sheepskin, for example, naturally reflected the shape of the animal. Cuneiform tablets are also rectangular when viewed from above. It seems that humans reconfigure their natural environment by making it rectangular.

Nevertheless, surprisingly few rectangular objects exist within nature with the exception of some mineral crystals, which are close to perfect cubes. Modern science is, as we are well aware, built on the order discovered in nature, so it isn't strange to find the mathematical principle of the square concealed there. Yet squares and rectangles are extremely unstable, which explains why they are so rare. Why then have people come to favor rectangular forms? One possibility is the fact that, if we break a big leafy

and opaque.

The physical standard of white, the so-called "degree" of whiteness, is not an indicator of how we perceive white. Accordingly, a higher degree of whiteness alone does not shape our impression. Our experience of the whiteness of flowers blooming in riotous profusion is diminished when a sheet of photocopy paper is placed in the background. The faint white of their petals is heavy with moisture. But we perceive the whiteness of their glorious blossoms as striking. In short, white is a phenomenon that arises from within our sensitivity.

The construction of a book is based on a repetitive rumination on white, involving the eye, the fingertips, and memory. When designing a book, we begin with a dummy sample, a book of blank, white pages. This is, so to speak, an architectural image made of paper, and I have erected such edifices countless times. Perhaps, like the white flowers, information is a product of the collaboration between such experimental acts and the unconscious. I think this process underlies my perceptions as a designer.

White Square Paper

> a white square
> within it
> a white square
> within it
> a white square
> within it
> a white square
> within it
> a white square
> within it

This verse, taken from a four-part poem, "Monotonous Space" (*Tancho na Kukan*) written by Kitasono Katsue (1902-1978), conveys an image that is extraordinarily white. A white square appears which is whiter than the one that preceded it. Then within it another white square appears which is whit-

cloudy sky, that looks as soft and deep as a carpet, or as hard as a board, or as light as air, or malleable, or sturdy ... The list goes on and on. Therefore, although it may look easy at first, choosing paper for a book is invariably a long and difficult process, since it involves the bringing together of these many "whites." We must find a balance between "reddish whites," "bluish whites," and "yellowish whites," and decide on the proper length and thickness of the fiber. Then each part of the book can play its proper role: the front cover conveys a powerful silence; the inside cover the purity of first openings; the title page the texture of new beginnings; while the body of the text sets the words and pictures against a clear background, or whispers "touch me!" to the reader's fingertips.

White steps forward or back in relation to the colors surrounding it. The reason it may appear more or less "white" is not physical; rather, it is contrast that causes it to appear brighter, fade into the background, or seem dull. Paper today is a manufactured product, and there are established standards by which its whiteness is measured. Carbonated magnesium – the white powder we see gymnasts rubbing on their hands before performing on the parallel bars – is one of these. Although it has long been the measure of whiteness, however, in recent years an even whiter paper has been developed that does not have the bluish tinge of fluorescent lighting but is purely white. This whiteness stands out when it is set against other sheets of white paper. Thus we use it when we want to accentuate whiteness.

At a certain point I came to the realization that merely using the whitest paper does not yield the strongest impression of whiteness. In fact, a book which uses pure white alone leaves a much weaker impression than a book in which careful attention is paid to the shades of white used for the cover, the book-band, the inside cover, the main text, and so on. Perhaps this is because the human eye adapts so quickly to shades of light and dark. It is rather when our senses must assess degrees of transparency and weight that the full orchestration of whiteness occurs, and the maximum affect is achieved. A sense of white's depth is evoked when a semi-transparent glassine paper is superimposed on a matte white with the texture of eggshells. Or we can be startled by white's sublime clarity when, while flipping through mirror-like sheets of glossy paper, we encounter a white that is plaster-like

great disparities, which mattered. That way, the tapestry would be far more delicate. As the variety of colors I encountered on the street soared, as the template of hues available to put on paper or on my computer increased from the hundreds into the thousands, the less I found myself interested in the diversity of colors. I therefore came to place only the most basic and necessary materials on my worktable, a decision that no doubt shaped my work. Then, at some point, color itself became redundant and superfluous.

Of course color is culture, as I pointed out in my discussion of traditional colors. Black-and-white photographs are certainly beautiful, but their meaning would vanish were all color removed from the world. Nor am I arguing that artificial colors are ugly. To the contrary, I admire people who can exult in primary and other vivid colors. I am also fascinated by color computing's ability to manipulate pure color in the virtual world. Clearly, the normal practice of design precludes the omission of color. I am not one who particularly loves white, nor do I avoid the use of color. As a professional graphic designer, I use it every day. The only difference may be that, when I employ color, I am keenly conscious of the "functional" reasons for doing so. I understand that red is an appropriate color for emergency buttons and fire extinguishers; in short, that the logic underlying sign systems arises from our living environments.

Nevertheless, as I focused on subtle emotional and aesthetic distinctions in my work, I began to unconsciously turn away from the flood of artificial colors and towards the more unobtrusive realm of purely natural color. Rather than emphasizing the vivid and the bright, I found myself thrilling to the weathered color of old books, the grey of cardboard mixed with Japanese *washi* paper, and the delicate color of rust; I discovered reality and even a kind of kinship in the chic, natural colors of plant seeds and sand. Among all these things, that which left the greatest mark was the color white.

There are infinite kinds of white paper. Some are glossy, like the surface of a mirror, while others look as rough as sharkskin; some have a plaster-like, flat matte surface, while others have an eggshell-like texture; there are those that are shiny as if covered in talc, while others are as white as snow. We can also find white paper that has the ambiguous feel of a

to express themselves. Books can be understood as an important tool to carry this dialogue forward. When we delve into the meaning of the electronic media that surround us like air, then, mustn't we first revaluate their communicative, sensual power?

Ruminating on White

My job requires me to spend considerable time sitting in front of a computer typing. Even now I am tapping away on my keyboard. Yet I spend an equal amount of time in contact with paper. In the latter case, I can feel another part of my mind being activated, and a sudden increase in the amount of energy my brain is consuming. I have only to touch the tip of my pen or pencil to the paper for this to occur, but my response is intensified when my fingertips and eyes are involved; when I am selecting paper for a printing job, for example, or examining it during the bookmaking process. Perhaps it is more accurate to say that, rather than just touching the paper, I am ruminating on it. Usually, we use the word "ruminate" to refer to a cow repeatedly chewing and spitting up a cud of grass, but here I mean the repetitive process of considering and assessing images. I call up a number of images of white from memory, and then leisurely compare them to the actual sheets of white paper I have before me. "Ruminating" seems to fit this activity perfectly – it is much more accurate than "selecting" or "examining."

Book design begins with the bringing together of various kinds of white paper. You need one kind of paper for the frontispiece, another for the cover, another for the inside cover, another for the title page, and so on. Finally, there is the paper on which the main text itself is printed. In recent years, I have been using colored paper less and less. Why should white paper in particular have grabbed my attention? I was absorbed in the varieties of colored paper in the beginning, and mastered the vast range of hues found in the sample books; yet, at some point, I turned to white almost exclusively.

Design involves controlling differences. Yet, repeating the same jobs over and over taught me how important it is to limit those differences, retaining only those that are most essential. I came to believe that, if I wanted to weave a tapestry that was meaningful, it was narrow gradations, not

give it certain possibilities, which inspired the people who worked with it. The Stone Age lasted a surprisingly long time, and it is said that the shapes of such axes were passed down over a hundred thousand years. It is hard for us today to imagine how a single tool and its uses could remain basically unchanged for thousands of generations. Still, when we pick up such an object and feel its weight, hardness, and texture, we can instinctively understand the driving force behind its creation. Even now, I grow excited whenever I take such an object in hand. This excitement can be seen as the impulse that inspires all creative activity.

The Iron Age offers similar insights. The hard yet flexible quality of a medium such as iron can be seen as a catalyst for such activities such as agriculture and warfare. The feeling of plows and spades turning over the soil encouraged people to clear desolate land to establish peaceful settlements; while their ambitions to invade their neighbors, and their awareness of their power over life and death, were undoubtedly whetted by the sharpness of their swords of white steel.

The clay tablets and cuneiform script of the Babylonian period are yet another medium. The surface of these clay tablets was not always flat. In fact many are so swollen they seem about to burst, like notebooks billowing with documents. Their surfaces are jam-packed with tiny engraved cuneiform script. Why are these tablets so terribly warped? The reason is likely that they were supposed to be portable, and this design made it possible to squeeze in more words. In other words, the reason for the density of the lettering may have originated in a mentality that desired to maximize the usable surface; thus, the letters had to be small and the surface bent. We can deduce the power of this desire from the concrete object – the tablet itself, and the script that covers it. Culture is a reflection of human desire. If we compare this desire to the sail on a boat, then we can see the essential role of the wind – i.e. the given medium – that fills it. Such concrete "media" can always be found alongside culture and civilization.

The whiteness and resilience of paper have similarly stimulated human desire. Paper is not merely an inorganic material, a neutral surface used for printing letters and pictures. Rather, the qualities of paper have drawn people into an extended dialogue, which has enriched their capacity

nearly so rapidly. Nevertheless, even if it were accidental, paper's absence of color – its brilliant "whiteness" – and its taut "resilience" changed history. It was a breakthrough that evoked a primeval world of unblemished purity and calm, and an unprecedented sense of fulfillment. Its uniform thinness made it fragile and transient. Yet it preserved the intense "blackness" of the inked words and images. It was an event that marked the advent of a new and crucially important mode of perception, whose singular radiance illuminated the entire span of cultural history.

Today, the role that paper plays in our lives is being transformed by the growth of electronic media. The "Gutenberg Galaxy," we are told, is coming to an end. True, the world of communication created by the reciprocal relationship between paper and printing technology had the kind of explosive power that we associate with the creation of a galaxy. Yet to what extent has that galaxy been shattered? Although I appreciate the metaphor, the presumption that the electronic media have supplanted the world of paper and ink strikes me as far too narrowly conceived. Paper is much more than "writing material." Insofar as its "whiteness" symbolizes life and information, it is a catalyst that stimulates the mental processes of all human beings. Even had the invention of paper followed the development of electronic technology, I am convinced that the sheer act of holding a white piece of paper, so full of creative possibility, would bring about a surge of human imagination.

Paper as Creative Catalyst

Paper is often called "print media." This is especially true since the rise of electronic media, but unlike the electronic media, which intrinsically lack corporal substance, paper's basic nature cannot be fully grasped using the concept of "media."

When we look at culture and civilization from the standpoint of perception, we can find a catalyst in the surroundings of the people of the time that stimulates creative desire. In the case of Stone Age culture, for example, we only have to take a stone ax in hand to feel the creative drive of the person who made it at a gut level. Stone's weight and tactile quality

Inciting the Energy of *Itoshiroshi*

Paper is white. This statement may seem terribly obvious, yet paper's whiteness is far from ordinary. In fact, the invention of white paper can be seen as having cast a bright light over the course of human history. Yet because paper is so ubiquitous today, we take it entirely for granted, forgetting its special significance. As I argued in the previous chapter, white appears but rarely in daily life. Our imaginations have been incalculably altered as a result of having given that principle of whiteness material existence in the form of a thin, stiff sheet. Thus, although the invention of paper is generally described as the invention of "writing material," its practical application is less important than its "imaginative" impact. Certainly, paper is a form of media. Yet, while media are important for their functional uses, the degree to which they stimulate human creativity and communication is even more significant.

      Paper is the materialized energy of *itoshiroshi*, that extreme form of purity that is ladled out of chaos, and which appears to us as both potentiality and actuality. Human beings who come in contact with its latent potential are naturally driven to express themselves.

White as a Sheet of Paper

Paper was invented in China about two thousand years ago, during the later Han period. It is believed that its manufacture was systematized by a Chinese official named Sairin (Cai-Lun, 50-121). During this initial phase, paper was made by immersing shredded pieces of cloth in water, crushing them, and then scooping up the remnants with a sieve. Later, cloth was replaced by finely chopped tree bark. Although the original color of the bark was a light brown, or earth color, its fibers turned white during the last stages of the process. Paper's resilience is unlike that of any other material, and its texture is pleasant to touch with our fingertips. If its color were, let's say, the light green of young leaves, or the orange of a ripe persimmon, or if it had the softer consistency of vinyl, it is doubtful that the development of a culture based on writing and printing technology would have progressed

Chapter 2

Paper

and even alligators. Real life dwells within this white. The shell of the egg is like the membrane that forms the boundary between this world and the next, and when it breaks, what emerges is no longer white but imbued with the color of the animal. Is this not the moment when newborn life starts walking towards chaos?

When white emerges from boundless chaos, it becomes information, namely, life. Chaos is the "field," white is the "figure." The process of the emergence of figure from field is "creation." We can see all the basic forms layered in that imagination that apprehends white emerging from the chaos of grey.

perspective, life and information carry the same significance.

White can be seen as the basic form of life or information that emerges from chaos; it is that extreme form of negative entropy that is bound and determined to make a clean escape. Life radiates color, while the innate tendency of white is to escape color to reach the opposite side of chaos. Life comes into this world wearing white, but it begins to acquire color the instant it assumes concrete form and touches the earth, like a yellow chick emerging from a white egg. White can never be made manifest in the real world. We may feel that we have come into contact with white, but that is just an illusion. In the real world, white is always contaminated and impure. It is no more than a vestige, a sign pointing towards its origins. White is delicate and fragile. From the moment of its birth it is no longer perfectly white, and when we touch it we pollute it further, though we may not realize it. Yet, all the more because of this, it stands out clearly in our consciousness.

According to one of the most prominent experts in hieroglyphs, Shirakawa Shizuka (1910-2006), the Chinese characters for white「白」was modeled after the shape of the human skull. This is supposedly because the image of white held by the people who lived back then was based on the sight of abandoned skulls in the fields, bleached by wind, rain, and sunlight. Obviously, such unexpected encounters must have left their mark. The traces of life contained in the color white strikes us when we come upon animal bones in the desert, or shells along the seashore.

White exists on the periphery of life. Bleached bones connect us to death, but the white of milk and eggs, for example, speaks to us of life. Breast feeding is an important activity for all mammals, a way of passing life energy from parent to infant. Whether animal or human, milk is always white. When we say "milk white," though, our image is that of the organic entity, somehow muddied by the abundant, life-giving nutrition it contains. The taste of milk is the taste of milk white, the taste of this organic entity. I find it especially interesting that the life-giving liquid that streams from the breast is white in color.

Most eggs are white, regardless of the color of the birds who lay them. A white birds lays white eggs, but so do bluebirds, blackbirds, snakes,

sionist painters. Once joined, however, they immediately turn to the grey of chaos. Green leaves are tinged with scarlet and gold in the fall, only to wither away, just like the metaphor, "return to the soil." Yet chaos does not signify death. Rather it is filled with the energy of dazzling color, and will give birth to brand new colors once again.

We can place white within this realm of mutating and evolving life forms. White is the most singular and vivid image that arises from the center of chaos. It works against the principle of mixture, revealing itself by breaking the gravity that pulls everything towards grey. White is the most extreme example of this singularity. It is not a mixed entity; it is not even a color at all.

The second law of thermodynamics, entropy, conceptually demonstrates the nature of chaos. Its basic assumption is that the quantity of energy in the universe remains constant. For example, the temperature of hot coffee in a cup will soon drop to the temperature of its surroundings. As long as we hold the cup in our hand, the coffee will neither regain its heat nor freeze. Instead it will inevitably cool. This doesn't mean, though, that the heat has disappeared. Rather it has achieved a balance with its surrounding environment. The temperatures of Tokyo, Siberia, and the Congo basin are all different, thanks to the movements of the earth, which is like a living creature in itself. Yet over an immensely long period of time, all these places will come to share the same temperature. In a similar way, the temperature of the earth will gradually mix with that of the surrounding universe until, finally, the two will come to be the same. An increase in entropy means that singularity is being reduced as we move towards that inevitable endpoint. Just as all colors become grey through the process of mixture, so is the final destination of entropy a chaotic world filled with enormous energy. All heat – the temperature of a cup of coffee, of Tokyo, of the earth – is preserved within this grand balance. Yet this chaos does not imply death or nothingness. There always remains the possibility that the level of entropy will be reduced when this unidentifiable energy transforms itself into a singular form – call it life or information – which arises from chaos. Life is that which emerges from entropy's gravitational field. Information (meaning) emanates from the meaninglessness of chaos. From this

Traditional colors do not simply refer to the physical nature of light – as I mentioned earlier, they carry a diverse set of associations, both material and emotional. The fact that *ichijirushi* is latent in *shiro* helps explain its distinctive features, and makes it an extremely useful tool with which to analyze whiteness in greater depth.

Escaping Color

White is a particularly unusual color because it can also be seen as the absence of color. In the old days, Japanese referred to the latent possibilities that exist prior to an event taking place as *kizen*. Insofar as white contains the latent possibility of transforming into other colors, it can be seen as *kizen*.

White can be attained by blending all the colors of the spectrum together, or through the subtraction of ink and all other pigments. In short, it is "all colors" and "no color" at the same time. This identity as a color that can "escape color" makes white very special. Not only does white's texture powerfully evoke the materiality of objects; white can also contain temporal and spatial principles like *ma* (an interval of space and time) and *yohaku* (empty margin); or abstract concepts such as non-existence and zero.

Obviously, these attributes have nothing to do with white as a trendy consumable color, nor are they suitable topics for theoretical discussions about color. Neither can they be adequately discussed within the genealogy of traditional Japanese colors. Yet meditating on these aspects of white gives rise to a certain line of inquiry. If white is not simply a color, mightn't we be able to understand it as functioning like a design or expressive concept?

The Basic Form of Information and Life

The world is like a sumptuous feast of every imaginable color. The freshness of the trees, the sparkle of the surface of the water, the intense color of fruits, the fiery brilliance of a roaring bonfire – each and every one of these colors is dear to us. Yet, over a very long period of time, these infinite movements and palpitations of life mix together to form the color brown. The brilliance of nature's colors is as boisterous as the palettes of the Impres-

and modified by the Japanese according to their own sensibilities. A Japanese person was considered cultivated when he or she had gained a deep awareness of the beauty – expressed in the phrase "snow-moon-flower" – found in these seasonal changes, which were divided into five-day cycles.

Words which pinpoint the colors of the changing seasons, like *moegi-iro* ("the bright green of budding plants") or *asagi-iro* ("the greenish blue of the leaves of the leek"), are fragile, but they have the power to convince because they capture the moment of observation. This is why they enter us so deeply. The names of colors function like a thread attached to a frightfully slender needle, capable of stitching together our most delicate emotions. When the needle hits its target, we feel either pleasure or empathy. It can also strike us as very painful, since it makes us aware that this delicacy is disappearing from our modern living environment.

Just as a stalactite cave is formed through the accumulation of droplets that fall one by one in dizzying repetition over time, so mental images of the brilliance of nature or the changing world gradually accumulate to form the names of colors. Some things are lost and others transformed, but finally, without anyone being aware of it, color becomes established as a grand system of consciousness. There are probably as many traditional systems of color in this world as there are languages or cultures. "Traditional Japanese colors" is just one of these.

Itoshiroshi

The etymology of the word *shiro*, or white, one of the four traditional Japanese colors, is rooted in the ancient word *shiroshi*, which is in turn connected to the words *itoshiroshi* and *ichijirushi*. All of these terms are based on the corporeality of things. *Ichijirushi* is a clear and objective condition which manifests itself in the purity of light, the lucidity embodied in a drop of water, or the force of a crashing waterfall. *Shiroshi*, on the other hand, is the state of consciousness we enter when we focus on these things, when our senses seem to vibrate like the strings of a *koto*. Over a long history, these ancient words were absorbed into the concept of "white" or *shiro*, and established as an aesthetic principle.

them clear shape. We absorb the rightness of those linguistic choices at the emotional level. The way in which hues are perceived and savored is stored within a given culture under the rubric of "traditional colors."

When we try to imagine color, it may be necessary to erase from our minds all pre-established categories and return to a blank state. In fact the word *iro*, "color" in Japanese, also signifies "lover"; it contains a range of associations far broader than what color possesses today. The box of twelve crayons we are given to draw with when we are small children shapes our perception for better or for worse – it is from them that we garner concepts like "water color," "flesh color," and so on. But what if such parameters did not exist, and the words we had to describe color were far fewer? Would we see color the same way we do in today's world?

It is said that there were few color-related words in eighth-century Japan, when the first poetry collection, the *Manyoshu*, was published. The basic adjectives being used at that time were just four in number: *akai* (red); *kuroi* (black); *shiroi* (white); and *aoi* (blue). (By adding an "i," a noun becomes an adjective.) These four colors referred to: a state of brightness and energy (red); the absence of light (black); brilliance (white); and an impression of obscurity (blue). These four adjectives may strike us as too few, but in fact each word had a very broad range, and people were able to express subtle differences in meaning and atmosphere contextually. There was no need to classify colors as strictly as we do today, which means that blue and green, for example, could be lumped together emotionally, under the broader category of blue (*aoi*). Rather than communicating color through the use of adjectives, which rely on the psychology of the receiver, we can presume that they used the names of plant-based dyes such as indigo or violet, or the names of things like bitter orange, ashes, and young grass.

The numerous colors we call "traditional" originated in courtly Heian culture. People then had a delicate grasp of the changes within nature, and were able to express those changes through things like their clothes and household furnishings. This gave rise to a new form of culture, based on a shared aesthetic. A year is generally divided into four seasons, but the Chinese calendar system identified seventy-two characteristic weather patterns or *kou*, divided into twenty-four "seasons," a system which was adopted

themselves products of modern physics. The two most common methods of color classification are Munsell's and Ostwald's. In their systems, the three elements of color – value, chroma, and hue (in short, degrees of clarity and light) – can be explained by constructing a three-dimensional circular object which allows us to visualize the physical phenomenon (i.e. color) more easily. The object thus constructed, however, does not enable us to achieve a full sense of what we perceive as color. Things like the rich golden yellow of the yolk from a broken egg, or the color of tea brimming in a teacup, are not merely colors; rather they are perceived at a deeper level through their texture and their taste, attributes inherent in their material nature. People perceive color through the combination of such elements. In this regard, color is not understood through our visual sense alone, but through all our senses. Insofar as color systems are based solely on the physical, visual nature of objects, they cannot convey our total response.

Today we use sample books when selecting colors for printing, fabrics, and manufactured products. Most of their sample colors are standardized according to the systems developed by the aforementioned Munsell and Ostwald, which makes them very convenient and practical. Thanks to their orderliness and objectivity we are able to clearly distinguish one color from another.

Another sample book I often refer to is titled *Traditional Japanese Colors*, which is organized based on the old names Japanese used for colors. The purpose of this book is not systematic consistency, so we cannot always use it when precision is required. Rather its reputation is derived from the power it has to evoke one's imagination. Whenever I pick up this book, I can accept the nature of the color captured by the words smoothly and naturally. At the same time, my senses are awakened; I feel soothed as if hearing the dialect of my hometown, as well a tinge of loneliness. What is the source of these emotions?

It goes without saying that colors can reflect our delicate feelings. But that is not all. Can't we see the core of human emotion itself as arising from that moment when color was discovered? Colors do not exist separately and independently within nature; they are constantly shifting in response to subtle gradations of light. It is language that, magnificently, gives

White as Sensory Experience

There is no such thing as "white." Rather, "white" exists solely in our sensory perception. Therefore, we must not attempt to search for "white." Instead, we must search for a way to feel the whiteness. Through this process, we gain an awareness of a white that is slightly whiter than the white we experience normally. This in turn makes us aware of the surprising diversity of whiteness found in Japanese culture: we come to understand words such as silence and empty space, and distinguish the hidden meanings contained in them. As we achieve this rapport with white, our world glows more brightly, and its shadows deepen.

    The blackness of typescript doesn't mean that the letters are actually black; they merely appear black in contrast to a white sheet of paper. By the same token, the circle in the Japanese flag glows red only in relation to its white background. This relativity works in identical fashion with blue or beige as long as they are set against a white background. Because non-being longs for being, on occasion it creates a stronger sense of being than being itself. It is difficult to sustain the purity of white because it is so easily contaminated; its beauty strikes us with such power because of our painful awareness of its transience.

    Such things as Japanese architecture, the concept of space, book design and gardens were born in response to this mental process which interposes white. A similar way of approaching whiteness was proposed by Tanizaki Junichiro (1886-1965) in his essay, *In Praise of Shadow*, which interprets Japanese aesthetics from the standpoint of shadow. Tanizaki's idea of locating a vanishing point of a drawing using shadow is splendid. Yet can't there be another vanishing point; namely, that of extreme brightness contrasted with dark shadow?

What is Color?

Is white a color? It is like a color, yet at the same time we can also conceive of it as a non-color. What then, we must ask, is color in the first place?

    The mechanism of color has been organized into clear systems,

Chapter 1

The Discovery of White

| | Prologue | ii |

| Chapter 1 | The Discovery of White | 1 |

White as Sensory Experience / What is Color? /
Itoshiroshi / Escaping Color /
The Basic Form of Information and Life

| Chapter 2 | Paper | 11 |

Inciting the Energy of *Itoshiroshi* / White as a Sheet of Paper /
Paper as Creative Catalyst / Ruminating on White /
White Square Paper / Folding Language /
On Letters / Typeface and Typography

| Chapter 3 | Emptiness | 27 |

The Meaning of Emptiness / Hasegawa Tohaku's "Pine Trees" /
Emptiness as Limitless Potential /
Information and the Ise Shrine / Nothing is Said /
The Receptiveness of a Red Circle on a White Background /
Emptiness and White / The Tea Ceremony /
The Origins of the Japanese-style Room /
Thought Dwells in Emptiness /
Creative Questions Require no Answers

| Chapter 4 | Back to White | 47 |

Suiko and the Irreversible Text / A Leap toward White /
Cleaning / Defamiliarization / White Sand and Moonlight

| | Epilogue / Acknowledgements | 55 |

reflect the concept of emptiness. Although I initially began writing about "emptiness," however, before long I found myself discussing "white" – it was through a confrontation with the broad spectrum of "emptiness" that "white made its appearance. Linguistically speaking, the character for "white" (白 - *shiro*) occurs within the Japanese compound for "emptiness" (空白 - *kuhaku*); a connection that ultimately forced me to investigate the meaning of emptiness in terms of its relation to white. Correspondingly, I ended up writing about white first, and then moved on to emptiness.

It is my hope that, by the time you finish this book, "white" may look differently to you. If you can feel it radiating with a new and higher degree of clarity, then we can say that your senses have been refined. Such an elevated perception of white provides a condition which enables us to see our world in a brighter light.

Prologue

Kenya HARA

This book is not about color. Rather, I have attempted to investigate an entity called "white" in order to locate those resources of sensitivity that are posited by one's own culture. In other words, I have attempted to find the source of a Japanese aesthetic that produces simplicity and subtlety through the concept of white.

Designing is my job. My professional field is communication. This means I illustrate "circumstances" or "conditions" rather than making "things." I have shown my works in numerous exhibitions, and have produced countless posters, package designs, symbol marks, and book designs; products which all reflect the nature of my given "circumstance." My profession has led me to ponder how to create images that refresh, things so crystal clear as to leave a lasting impression. This intellectual process, in turn, made me begin paying attention to the means of cultural communication that have developed in Japan and, more broadly speaking, throughout the world. As this train of thought progressed, my sense that it was leading to new answers grew stronger and stronger.

"Emptiness" (*utsu*) and "completely hollow" (*karappo*) are among the terms I pondered while trying to grasp the nature of communication. When people share their thoughts, they commonly listen to each other's opinions rather than throwing information at each other. In other words, successful communication depends on how well we listen, rather than how well we push our opinions on the person seated before us. People have therefore conceptualized communication techniques using terms like the "empty vessel" to try to understand each other better. For example, unlike other signs whose meanings are narrowly determined, symbols like the cross or the red disk in the Japanese flag allow us to let our imaginations roam free of any boundaries; they are like enormous empty vessels that can hold every possible meaning. The concept of emptiness can be equally found in a cavernous mausoleum or church, or a small garden and tea house: all

WHITE

Kenya Hara

Chuokoron-Shinsha, Inc.